Love,
above the reach of time

Two Stories of The
Ladies of Llangollen*

* lang - goff - lan

Welsh is an explosively expressive language. The main difficulty in pronouncing Llangollen is the double "l" at its beginning. Two phonetic descriptions which may help in pronunciation of the double "l" are:

1. as "th" - thang - goff - lan

2. as if you are starting to say "laugh," but use only the "l" sound, not the word - lhang -goff - lan

Love,
above the reach of time[*]

Two Stories of The
Ladies of Llangollen

Anna M. Curren

*From a sonnet written for The Ladies by
William Wordsworth: "To the Lady E.B. and
the Hon. Miss P. Composed in the grounds
of Plass Newidd 1824; published 1827."

LadyePress
U.S.A.

Books are available at special quantity discounts for fund
raising and related purposes.

EDITOR: Alice Taylor Hanson

BOOK DESIGNERS: Peter T. Noble Associates, Encinitas,
CA

COVER PAINTING: Jane Morris Pack, Paros, Greece

SCREENPLAY ILLUSTRATION: Mark G. Willems

PHOTO CREDITS: The National Library of Wales.
Aberystwyth, Dyfed; Mike Flory. Used by permission
of Glyndwr District Council, Ruthin, Clwyd, Wales;
Laurie D. Munday; Elliott Framan; Rick Starkman
Photography, San Diego, Ca

PRINTING: Ty Wood Printing, Sun Valley, CA

Published by LadyePress U.S.A.
P.O. Box 34662
San Diego, CA 92163-4662
858.488.2866

www.ladyepress.com

142753

Manufactured in The United States of America

4   3   2   1

OCT 0 6 2001 A

Fade In

*L*ove, above the reach of time is an unusual book, about a very unusual love, a deeply passionate love that developed over two hundred years ago, and endured through countless difficulties for over fifty years. So spectacular was this love that it made its participants famous throughout Great Britain, Europe, and most of the English speaking world. It is a book which tells both the fictional and real love story of two unique and amazing women, and in so doing it attests that love, the most intense and universal of all human experiences, is in no way altered by sexual orientation or gender identity.

My story about this particular romance started because of an offhand comment made by a friend during a visit to Wales, which included the home of The Ladies of Llangollen, in 1993. I had been obsessed for over a year with the desire to write a love story about two women in the form of an original motion picture screenplay, a desire which was unshakable, in spite of the fact that although I had been a successful author for over 20 years, I was totally ignorant of screenwriting techniques. My friend suggested I write my screenplay about "these two Ladies." The seed thus planted, from that moment on The Ladies have seldom been out of my thoughts.

The original screenplay about The Ladies, which I completed in 1996, was judged by those in the film industry who reviewed it as a "good read," the ultimate compliment which can be paid an original script. However, from the first I also saw the work as a book, a desire which was put on hold when my screenplay was optioned for production by the first company I submitted it to. This option expired after a year, due to the producers not having obtained financing for the film. A not unusual event, I have since learned, for an original work, particularly for the subject matter I had chosen. So I began to rethink publication.

I wanted to do this book about The Ladies because there were so many pieces of the story which could not be told in a film. While the screenplay includes many real characters and facts, it is ultimately a work of fiction. Thus it leaves untold most of the details of the real story which inspired the work. In writing *Love, above the reach of time* I have thus added the remarkable love story which so inspired my screenplay, as well as some of the salient facts of my own journey in completing it.

Publication will also provide a wonderful opportunity to make the original script available to a broad professional audience, which it has never had, because I have never sought the assistance of an agent.

Reading *Love, above the reach of time* provides each reader a unique opportunity to experience those features in the first reading of an original script which attract actors, directors and producers to it. So, now it's time for me to invite you to turn the page, and begin your dual journeys with the unforgettable Ladies of Llangollen. Enjoy.

A Review of the Misbeliefs about Female Sexuality Current in The Ladies' Lifetime

*A*ll existing beliefs about female sexuality were abruptly shattered a little over 200 years ago in the spring of 1778. The news of the unprecedented elopement of two Anglo-Irish noblewomen, Lady Eleanor Butler and The Honorable Miss Sarah Ponsonby, electrified a staid and genteel British society which had been basking in the status quo of sexual misinformation and ignorance. In short order the elopement became heady gossip, which spread rapidly throughout not only the British Isles and Europe, but ultimately to many other parts of the English speaking world.

While Eleanor and Sarah's elopement precipitated a quiet revolution in the recognition of same sex relationships between women, it also had a major impact on the understanding of female sexuality per se. To place this revolution in perspective, a review of the beliefs about female sexuality current at the time of the elopement is enlightening. The marriage practices of the upper gentry and nobility provide a logical beginning point, which is the class to which both Eleanor and Sarah belonged.

Marriage in 1778 was not primarily motivated by love, but by property. Thus the first consideration in matchmaking, the romantic novels of Jane Austen notwithstanding, was the securing or protection of property and/or titles, or, in the best case scenario, both. This ensured that in most cases the partners in a marriage had no emotional attachment to each other, nor did they expect to develop one. Procreation was a necessary duty to ensure the continuation of the system, and affection, if it did develop, would most likely have been far removed from today's expected norm. In short, upper gentry women were traded breeders, often married to men they had no or perhaps even negative feelings toward, and with whom they may also have had little social intercourse in their daily lives.

With servants available to raise the offspring of these unions, upper class women, deprived of emotional fulfillment, began to find it in each others' company. Thus evolved what was referred to as the Age of Romantic Feminism, which was in full bloom at the time of Eleanor and Sarah's elopement. Romantic feminism describes a period in which it was common for upper class women, both married and unmarried, to develop passionately close relationships with other women. When physically together these couples, which the partners in romantic friendships were recognized to be, were inseparable, publicly swooned in each other's arms, shared a common bed, and in every sense were the primary emotional focus of each others' lives. When separated they communicated via countless endearing letters, and by writing and sometimes publishing poetry for their chosen which occasionally bordered on the erotic. These relationships were, understandably, subject to predictable heartache and depression when they were terminated, either by a change of affection, or in many cases, marriage. And, while it is likely that most romantic friendships did not involve a sexual relationship, it certainly provided women who had a lesbian orientation ample opportunity to form passionate covert sexual attachments in the public arena.

What did upper class men think of these romantic friendships? This was an era in which they widely embraced the misconception that upper class women were incapable of achieving orgasm, often referred to as "venereal orgasm." Orgasm was considered an erotic response limited to "bad" women in the lower classes, which included actresses, who were not awarded the professional status they enjoy today. Indeed, absence of orgasm may have been the prevailing response of upper class wives in what were probably loveless and sexually ignorant couplings. Thus romantic friendships were perceived by upper class males to be sexually innocent, and in fact were generally thought admirable.

Were upper class men ignorant of the possibility of female same sex relationships? Homosexuality had been widely recognized in men for centuries, and was at the time a criminal and punishable offense in Great Britain. However, same sex relationships between women were normally dismissed as a physical impossibility, because penile penetration was thought an absolute necessity in the sexual act. This further led to romantic friendships being viewed, especially between married women, with a sense of security. For if women were devoted to other women there was small likelihood of their becoming attracted to other men, which would have presented a definite threat in the marriage stakes.

In this age of romantic feminism a number of cohabiting upper class female couples, who are today identified as lesbians, were naively believed to have had no "genital component" in their relationships, as if somehow these committed couples had transcended the physical needs of mere mortals, or were incapable of discovering acts of loving on their own. So pervasive was this attitude in many minds that Eleanor and Sarah were facetiously and famously dubbed "The Most Celebrated Virgins in Europe," a designation which stuck in spite of obvious evidence to the contrary.

Their public designation of virginity notwithstanding, Eleanor and Sarah's relationship was from the very beginning viewed by many with great suspicion. They themselves added fuel to this suspicion in their post elopement lives together by openly declaring and demonstrating their love for each other. They referred to each other always in such revealing terms as "my beloved" or "my better half." They made no secret of the fact that they shared the same bed but, as would be expected, they neither talked nor wrote about the sexual aspects of their lives. However, in a recently discovered diary of one of their most intimate friends, Mrs. Hester Thrale Piozzi, a renowned literary figure of that era, The Ladies are described as "damned Sapphists." Mrs. Piozzi further adds the prejudicial claim that unaccompanied women felt unsafe to spend an overnight visit with them. Thus Eleanor and Sarah's elopement initiated a dramatic change in the perception of female sexuality. It revealed a depth of emotional and sexual possibilities which could not have failed to threaten the innocence romantic friendships had previously been afforded.

The Piozzi reference, and other fascinating facts about lesbian relationships between 1663 to 1801, were extensively documented in 1994 by Emma Donoghue (now Dr. Donoghue) in her excellent book, *Passions Between Women*. Her research of British literature revealed that there was surprisingly wide lesbian information available to all levels of society, much of it understandably erroneous, such as the belief that only a prolapsed uterus or abnormally large clitoris could substitute for a penis to make female same sex possible. Therefore, it is not unreasonable to assume that upper class women, who were better educated than most of their sex, were particularly knowledgeable of same sex possibilities. This, of course, would have included Eleanor and Sarah, who were of noble lineage.

Within a year of their elopement Eleanor and Sarah had settled in the small village of Llangollen, Wales, where they began the publicly committed and loving relationship that lasted for over 50 years. Their relationship indisputably establishes them as the first internationally famous lesbian couple: The Ladies of Llangollen.

The real facts of Eleanor and Sarah's separate and collective lives give witness to the truth of the old adage that fact is stranger than fiction. *Love, above the reach of time,* the original screenplay about The Ladies which follows, portrays Eleanor and Sarah as the lovers they indisputably were. Although this period screenplay incorporates some of the actual facts of The Ladies' incredible lives, it is, of necessity, a work of fiction.

One of the most amazing facts of Eleanor and Sarah's lives is the number of famous people who sought them out in Llangollen and became intimate friends. Among these were famous writers such as Sir Walter Scott; poets such as Lord Byron and William Wordsworth; scientists and physicians such as Sir Humphry Davy and Dr. Robert W. Darwin (father of Charles); and countless of the nobility and political figures of their era, in particular Arthur Wellesley, the Duke of Wellington, who became a close personal and lifelong friend. You will meet these and other famous friends in the opening scene of the screenplay, which takes place in 1815 at Plas Newydd, The Ladies' home in Llangollen, as they host a party to celebrate the victory of their friend Arthur, the Duke of Wellington, over Emperor Napoleon Bonaparte of France.

To get you started an explanation of a few abbreviations used in screenplays is in order: EXT identifies an exterior setting, while INT an interior; three periods (an ellipse) indicate a pause in the dialogue, and two dashes that the speaker is interrupted; VO is narration which tells the thoughts of the character; SUPER is the superimposition of a title on a film frame; and CU indicates a close up shot. Each scene identifies a specific location and the characters in it, whose names are capitalized the first time they appear in the film. As the screenplay progresses the characters' dialogue reveals their personalities, hopes, fears and dreams, as the story proceeds to its dramatic conclusion.

Love,
above the reach of time

The Screen Story of The
Ladies of Llangollen

an original screenplay by
Anna M. Curren

The Players

The Ladies Of Llangollen

Lady Eleanor Butler of Kilkenny, Ireland; and
The Honorable Miss Sarah Ponsonby of Innistiogue, Ireland.

Famous Friends In The Opening Scene

Arthur Wellesley, The Duke of Wellington Most famous for his defeat of the French Emperor Napoleon Bonaparte at Waterloo, 1815. Always a soldier, and in later life a statesman.

Emperor Napoleon Bonaparte Not at the party, but referred to in conversation several times. The defeated Emperor was already imprisoned on the island of St. Helena, where he remained until his death.

Sir Humphry Davy One of England's greatest early scientists in the fields of electricity and chemistry. First Director of the scientific Royal Institute of Great Britain. Discoverer of the elements potassium and sodium, inventor of the miner's safety lamp.

Sir Walter Scott Renowned and much loved Scottish author. His innovative writing style popularized historical novels by making his characters so real and human that readers could share the excitement of their lives and the events portrayed.

Dr. Robert Darwin A much respected English physician. His father Erasmus was the first evolutionary biologist.

Charles Darwin Son of Dr. Robert Darwin, age seven at the time of the party, Charles followed in his grandfather's scientific footsteps, producing the controversial *Origin of Species*.

Lord Byron One of Great Britain's most famous poets and statesmen. A definite ladies' man, he has brought his latest conquest to the party.

Lady Caroline Lamb Lord Bryon's current mistress. A titled married woman, her life was destroyed when Bryon subsequently moved on to other romantic conquests.

William Wordsworth A renowned English poet, famous for the romanticism he introduced in his works. A close friend of The Ladies, he wrote poetry about and for them.

Eleanor's Family

Sir Walter Butler Her father. A gentle man somewhat overpowered by his wife.

Lady Butler Eleanor's mother. A stong, opinionated woman, to say the least.

Sarah's Family

Lady Betty Fownes Sarah's cousin, a sweet-natured frail noblewoman.

Sir William Fownes Lady Betty's husband. Not at all sweet-natured. One of the villains of the play, and of Sarah's real life.

The Other Players - will introduce themselves.

Read on.

The Screenplay

EXT. PLAS NEWYDD - DAY - 1815

The Ladies of Llangollen, LADY ELEANOR BUTLER, 62, and the HONORABLE MISS SARAH PONSONBY, 56, are entertaining GUESTS on the lawn of their modest two story manor house. They are hosting the party to celebrate the victory over the Emperor Napoleon by their friend, THE DUKE OF WELLINGTON, 45, who is attired in military uniform. They look strikingly beautiful in modest but fashionable gowns. The guests include SIR HUMPHRY DAVY, 34, scientist, and LADY DAVY, 41; DR. DARWIN, 47, MRS. ROBERT DARWIN, 43, and son CHARLES DARWIN, 7; the Scottish LORD BYRON, 25, who has a lame left leg, and his beautiful new mistress, LADY CAROLINE LAMB, 33; the Scottish writer SIR WALTER SCOTT, 42, and his wife CHARLOTTE; and the Poet WILLIAM WORDSWORTH, 43. A VIOLINIST is playing period music as a modestly dressed male SERVANT and MAID are serving wine and appetizers from a festively decorated table.

SUPER: PLAS NEWYDD, LLANGOLLEN, WALES - 1815

The Ladies introduce their guests to the Duke of Wellington.

ELEANOR
> Sir Humphry and Lady Davy, The Duke of Wellington. You'll remember that Emperor Napoleon presented Sir Humphry with a medal for his discoveries at the Royal Scientific Institute, Duke. How do you feel about the defeat of your hero, Humphry?

DAVY
> He's no hero of mine, Lady Eleanor. It was the French scientific community that honored me. I could see in his eyes that he understood nothing of it.

DUKE OF WELLINGTON

I've long admired your work, Sir Humphry.

DAVY

Unlikely as much as we welcomed yours, Duke. Our very society depended on it.

DUKE OF WELLINGTON

A bit of an overstatement, perhaps.

LADY DAVY

Not in the least. You have no idea how terrified we felt here at home.

SARAH

Lady Davy isn't exaggerating. The country lived in constant fear of invasion. You'll have to get used to being a hero, Arthur.

DUKE OF WELLINGTON

Thank you, Sarah, but luck played its part. Fame is very much dependent on opportunity, I now realize.

ELEANOR

Don't depreciate your victory, Arthur. Your new troop support system had more to do with victory than either luck or opportunity.

The novelist SIR WALTER SCOTT and his wife CHARLOTTE have approached and wait to be introduced.

SARAH

Don't be shy in introducing yourselves, Sir Humphrey. Many here are anxious to meet you.

ELEANOR

Sir Walter and Lady Charlotte Scott.

Sir Walter grasps the Duke's extended hand in both of his, and shakes it vigorously.

SCOTT

Well done, man, well done! 'Tis proud we are to meet you.

CHARLOTTE

He's talked of nothing else for weeks.

DUKE OF WELLINGTON

Lady Eleanor and Miss Ponsonby can verify that I'm equally as pleased to meet you, Sir Walter. Your splendid book *Ivanhoe* has traveled with me on all my campaigns.

ELEANOR

Wait until you read his latest, Arthur, *The Bride of Lammermoor*. Destined to be an opera if ever a novel was.

SCOTT

Perceptive of you to think so, Eleanor. Charlotte's thoughts run along similar lines. Not a connection I made myself, I must confess.

SARAH

Have you talked with Lord Byron yet? He expressly wished to meet you.

SCOTT

We're on our way, if you'll excuse us.

The Scotts move away as the Ladies and Duke continue to stroll.

ELEANOR

People will be writing about you soon, Arthur. Better be prepared.

DUKE OF WELLINGTON

It's already started. I'd rather be left alone.

SARAH

No chance of that. Defeating Napoleon sealed your fate.

ELEANOR

And fame.

DUKE OF WELLINGTON

But you two are more famous than I. Name anyone who is intimate with more notables than you?

ELEANOR

Ah! But we've done nothing to be remembered for. The curiosity we've inspired won't survive, while your achievements will.

SARAH

Being blessed with the intimacy of so many
interesting people has been fame enough for us.

ELEANOR

(teasing)
Speak for yourself, Sarah. It invites the curious,
Duke, not always pleasant.

DUKE OF WELLINGTON

Must you keep calling me "Duke?"

SARAH

Of course we must. You've earned it, and it's your
day to celebrate. Here come the Darwins. Their son
Charles will have a million questions for you. He's
a true prodigy.

DR., MRS. and son CHARLES DARWIN approach.

ELEANOR

Dr. and Mrs. Darwin, the Duke of Wellington.

DR. DARWIN

A great privilege for both Mrs. Darwin and myself.
Our congratulations, Duke.

CHARLES DARWIN

(pulling on Eleanor's dress)
You haven't introduced *me*, Eleanor.

ELEANOR

Give me a moment, Charles, for goodness' sake! I've
warned the Duke about your precociousness, and
we're going to let you have him entirely to yourself for
a few minutes.

SARAH

Make the time count, Charles. This is a busy day for
our friend.

The Ladies move away.

ELEANOR

Let's find Byron. This isn't likely to be the most
popular day of his career.

SARAH

If he chooses to break up a respectable marriage
and openly parade his new mistress what else can he
expect?

They are stopped briefly by several guests as they make their way to LORD BYRON, who is standing alone.

BYRON

I'm glad you made time for me, Ladies. I feel like a pariah.

SARAH

You enjoy notoriety, Byron. Don't expect sympathy.

ELEANOR

(shaking her head)
Your attraction for the opposite sex totally mystifies me. How do you do it?

BYRON

I'm charming and irresistible. Why else do *you* keep inviting me to visit?

SARAH

It's your *mind* we love, Byron. I, especially, have reservations about your morals.

BYRON

Then don't think about them.

LADY CAROLINE LAMB joins them, and Byron, smiling, instantly entwines her arm in his, and covers her hand with his.

ELEANOR

Welcome, Caroline. How are you weathering the storm?

LADY CAROLINE

Quite well, actually. We English are too well bred to be blatantly rude.

She looks adoringly at Byron, who returns the exchange, and kisses her lightly on the cheek.

LADY CAROLINE

It was kind of you to include me in the invitation. I thank you both.

They are joined by the Duke of Wellington, who shakes hands with Byron, and nods to acknowledge Lady Caroline.

SARAH

You know Lord Byron, Arthur, but I don't think you've met Lady Caroline Lamb.

DUKE OF WELLINGTON
Lady Caroline, a pleasure. I've heard of you, of course.

LADY CAROLINE
Has anyone *not* heard of me?

DUKE OF WELLINGTON
(embarrassed, turns to Byron)
I didn't have an opportunity to congratulate you on your first speech in the House, Byron. It was brilliant.

BYRON
(musing)
It seems I can talk as well as write. A bit of a surprise to me.

ELEANOR
Not to me. You're unreasonably talented, my friend.

BYRON
Is that supposed to be a compliment?

SARAH
I think you may accept it as one.

BYRON
But this is your day, Arthur. Our congratulations for ending the turmoil. What's he really like, this Napoleon?

DUKE OF WELLINGTON
A strutting little peacock. Not a shred of guilt at having starved his troops on their retreat, yet they worshipped him. Beyond my understanding.

BYRON
(to The Ladies)
Have you talked with Wordsworth yet?

SARAH
No, why do you ask?

BYRON
He's written a new poem for you. He's been reading it to everyone he can persuade to listen.

ELEANOR
There he is. Let's see what this is all about. Excuse us, Arthur.

8

The Ladies walk to an area where the poet WILLIAM WORDSWORTH has the attention of 5 or 6 guests.

SARAH

What's this we hear about a poem, William?

WORDSWORTH

A new poem to honor you, Ladies.

ELEANOR

(teasing)

Improved over your last attempt, I hope, Wordsworth.

WORDSWORTH

Let's see what you think.

"A stream to mingle with your favorite Dee,
Along the Vale of Meditation flows;
Pleased to see in Nature's face, Expression of repose.
In ours the Vale of Friendship, let this spot
Be named, where faithful to a low roofed Cot
On Deva's banks, ye have abode so long,
Sisters in love, a love allowed to climb
Even on this earth, above the reach of time!"

ELEANOR

(deeply touched)

Much better. But "low roofed cot?" You pay little tribute to our beautification of Plas Newydd, William.

WORDSWORTH

(laughing)

You're wonderful, Eleanor. No chance of my doing poor work with a critic like you at hand.

SARAH

Don't listen to her, William. I think it's lovely. "Sisters in love..."

She looks lovingly at Eleanor, and reaches to take her hand.

ELEANOR

How little we dreamed...

DISSOLVE

EXT. AERIAL VIEW OF A BLIND CURVE ON A DIRT ROAD IN LUSH GREEN COUNTRYSIDE - DAY

SUPER - NEAR KILKENNY IRELAND 1765

Three horsemen, LORD WALTER BUTLER, in his 40s, 18 year old SIR GEOFFREY BANNISTER, and LADY ELEANOR BUTLER, 13 years old, dressed in groom's riding attire including a cap which completely covers her long hair, rapidly approach the curve from one direction as a carriage, bearing a DRIVER, MAID, LADY CROWTHER and her TWO CHILDREN, aged 4 and 5, approaches from the opposite direction.

EXT. CURVE IN ROAD - DAY

The horsemen round the curve and almost crash headlong into the carriage. The carriage horse, startled, rears up and tosses the driver from his seat, then veers sharply off the road toward the steep precipice of a rapidly flowing river. Eleanor reacts immediately, turns her horse and gallops after the runaway carriage. The passengers scream as Eleanor catches the horse by its bridle, and slows it gently to a stop. In the rescue her cap has been blown off, revealing her long hair. As the pandemonium eases, Lord Walter rides quickly up to the coach, where the maid and Lady Crowther try to calm the wildly crying children.

LADY CROWTHER
Oh, dear God! Lord Walter, is that you?

LORD WALTER
Lady Crowther! Are you unharmed?

Lady Crowther, already in a state of shock, is even more shocked to recognize that it is Eleanor who has stopped the runaway.

LADY CROWTHER
Eleanor? Is that Lady Eleanor?

LORD WALTER
Yes, indeed it is, Lady Crowther. And a lucky thing it is she came along today. I no longer have the quickness to do what she did.

LADY CROWTHER

(mystified, in spite of her distress)
But I've never heard Lady Butler talk of Eleanor
riding.

LORD WALTER

An oversight, I'm sure. Eleanor so seldom has the
time.

*Geoffrey rides up with the carriage driver mounted behind him.
They dismount and the driver climbs shakily back in the carriage
and picks up the reins. Geoffrey goes immediately to Eleanor,
who has dismounted to retrieve her cap.*

LADY CROWTHER

(angrily to Lord Walter)
We might all have been killed by your recklessness.

LORD WALTER

It was hardly that, Lady Crowther. I've never seen
a horse react so skittishly. I have great concern over
your continuing to use him.

LADY CROWTHER

Nonsense! It was your fault entirely. You were riding
insanely.

LORD WALTER

I'm not prepared to argue over this, Lady Crowther.
I'm as entitled to an opinion based on my experience
as you are to yours. The important thing is that
no one has been injured, thanks to Eleanor's quick
action. This is what we must remember, don't you
agree?

*Lady Crowther looks sullenly and angrily at Lord Walter and
Eleanor, then turns away in disgust.*

LADY CROWTHER

Drive on, Michael.

GEOFFREY

We'd best be off too, Sir Walter. Good day, Lady
Crowther.

SIR WALTER

Right you are, Geoffrey. Ready, Eleanor?

*Eleanor has retrieved and replaced her cap. She and Geoffrey
remount quickly.*

ELEANOR
Good day, Lady Crowther.

All ride off in their original directions.

GEOFFREY
Take my coat, Eleanor, you're shivering.

ELEANOR
Thank you, Geoffrey... This will be the end of it, father.

LORD WALTER
Damn! I've taken such care to avoid discovery. Perhaps she'll say nothing. You did save their lives after all.

ELEANOR
Not a chance. She has a tongue to match her temper. This will bring repercussions.

EXT. KILKENNY CASTLE - DAY

A coach bearing a smug faced Lady Crowther drives away from the Castle.

INT. DRAWING ROOM/CASTLE - DAY

LADY BUTLER looks out the window as Lord Walter enters. Several ugly and poorly painted portraits hang on the walls.

LADY BUTLER
How dare you let Eleanor dress as a boy and ride!

LORD WALTER
She saved their lives!

LADY BUTLER
You're the cause of this, Walter. You've made me the laughing stock of Kilkenny. Eleanor's behavior has always been inappropriate, and you encourage her. Well, I intend to put a stop to it once and for all.

SIR WALTER
We anticipated you'd forbid her riding.

LADY BUTLER
Forbid her riding? Oh, no. This escapade demands much stronger action. She refuses to learn social graces from me, so I'll arrange for her to learn them elsewhere.

LORD WALTER
And what elsewhere did you have in mind?

LADY BUTLER
A convent. Cambria, I think.

LORD WALTER
France! But surely there are convents here in Ireland that will do?

LADY BUTLER
Not with the reputation of this one. Eleanor's education is my responsibility. I'll make any decision I feel appropriate for her.

Lady Butler forestalls Lord Walter's attempt to protest.

LADY BUTLER
How can I arrange a favorable marriage for her if she doesn't learn to conform? No, no, no! I'm resolute in this decision, Walter, and I won't discuss it further. Tell Eleanor my intentions any way you see fit.

INT. ELEANOR'S BEDROOM - DAY

The room is very plainly furnished. Eleanor stands reading a book when A KNOCK sounds and the door opens.

ELEANOR
Father! Come in.

LORD WALTER
Lady Crowther has just visited.

ELEANOR
I know. And I'm sure mother has treated you abominably. I'm sorry your kindness to me is always repaid with her anger.

LORD WALTER
It's of no account, I'm used to it. In her heart she means well... I have an important matter to discuss with you, Eleanor.

ELEANOR
(alarmed)
You look so grave. What is it, father?

LORD WALTER

Your mother is determined to send you to a convent in France. To teach you discipline.

Eleanor comprehends, and reacts with happiness.

ELEANOR

France! I can't believe it! And a chance to study. But this is wonderful news. It makes me sorry we weren't discovered sooner.

LORD WALTER

(surprised, but sad)

I'm relieved it pleases you, but it concerns me. You're very young to be so far from home. And I'm selfish. What will I do without you? My life will be joyless.

ELEANOR

Leaving you will be my only regret, father. Mother hates me so.

LORD WALTER

You're wrong, Eleanor. Your mother is only interested in preparing you for your station in life, but you try her patience with your resistance. She hopes the Sisters will succeed where she feels she's failed.

ELEANOR

But the life she wishes on me is so boring! Embroidery, needlepoint, gossip. All useless!

SIR WALTER

Social conventions *must* be observed, Eleanor. In time you'll see your mother is right.

ELEANOR

But France! Just think of it, father. I can write and tell you all the wonderful things I'm learning. Please be as happy for me as I am for myself.

LORD WALTER

I'll try, Eleanor. I will try.

She hugs her father spontaneously, and he responds sadly.

EXT. CASTLE - DAY

Eleanor's baggage is loaded into a coach as she stands beside it with her parents. The Castle grounds look grim and untended, without flowers or color.

EXT. COUNTRY CEMETERY - DAY

*A PRIEST intones blessings at a grave side where several
MOURNERS and a frail SARAH PONSONBY, 13, clutches
a well used and worn Bible, and weeps. Two MAIDS whisper
nearby.*

MAID # 1
Poor Miss Sarah. To lose her mother at 5, now her
father at 13. The stepmother won't have her. What's
to become of her?

MAID # 2
Being sent to a cousin in Inistiogue, I hear. Lady
Betty Fownes. Not a happy place, rumor has it.

MAID # 1
How so?

MAID # 2
The husband is a devil. He treats her ladyship very
poorly.

*The service concludes and Sarah walks to a waiting coach. The
maids go to bid her farewell.*

MAID # 1 and 2
Good luck, Miss Sarah. God bless.

SARAH
(trying to control her grief and fear)
Thank you, you've been so kind. I won't forget you.

The maids wave as the coach gets under way.

EXT. WOODSTOCK - DAY

*A large Georgian home in Inistiogue, situated on a pretty hillside
surrounded by beautiful gardens. Sarah's coach stops in front of
the house, and she tentatively exits. Her cousin, LADY BETTY
FOWNES, a charming, warm, fluttery, sweet-spirited, but frail-
looking middle aged woman greets her effusively.*

LADY BETTY
Dear cousin Sarah. How happy I am to see you.
Welcome to your new home.

Lady Betty hugs the frightened child affectionately.

SARAH

How do you do, Lady Betty.

LADY BETTY

No need to be so formal, Sarah. I'd prefer you call me "cousin."

Lady Betty picks up Sarah's small bag, and with her arm over Sarah's shoulders, walks with her toward the house.

LADY BETTY

I'm so pleased you've come. Let me show you to your room, so you can begin to settle in.

INT. SARAH'S BEDROOM - DAY

A cheerful flowered bedspread brightens the room, which is large, sun filled and well furnished. Sarah stares around in wonder, walks tentatively forward, gently touching the bed, dressing table, and books on a well stocked bookshelf. She returns to stand mutely in front of Lady Betty.

LADY BETTY

How do you like it, Sarah?

SARAH

Oh, cousin, it's so beautiful!

She wraps her arms around Lady Betty, who smiles with relief and returns the embrace.

LADY BETTY

I'm so happy you like it. This was my very own daughter's room, but she's grown and married now. I've sorely missed my girl. But now, luckily, I'm to have another.

SARAH

I'll do anything you ask of me, cousin.

LADY BETTY

You must simply be yourself, Sarah! The only requirement is that you be happy.

A KNOCK sounds on the door, and a very young maid, MARY CARRYL, enters with a jug of hot water, which she places on a wash stand. She is followed by a WEST HIGHLAND WHITE PUPPY, which runs to Sarah, who delightedly scoops him up.

LADY BETTY

This is Mary Carryl, Sarah. She'll help you get settled. And Frisk, who seems to have decided he belongs to you. Come down when you're refreshed, my dear, and I'll show you the house and gardens. Later you'll meet Sir William, who's as eager to welcome you as I.

EXT. WOODSTOCK GARDEN - AFTERNOON

A refreshed and happy Sarah is in the garden with Lady Betty when a CARRIAGE IS HEARD APPROACHING.

LADY BETTY

That will be Sir William.

EXT. FRONT OF WOODSTOCK - AFTERNOON

The sullen faced but not unattractive middle aged SIR WILLIAM FOWNES disembarks from a chaise. He nods to Sarah, offers Lady Betty his arm, and all enter the house.

INT. DRAWING ROOM/WOODSTOCK - AFTERNOON

Sir William, Lady Betty and Sarah enter. Sir William immediately sits.

SIR WILLIAM

Sit. Sit. You've had a chance to look around, no doubt, Sarah. What do you think of our little Woodstock?

SARAH

It's the most beautiful house I've ever seen, Sir William.

Sir William, his face inscrutable, looks silently at Sarah.

SIR WILLIAM

Lady Betty is delighted to have you, and of course, so am I. But you must make an effort not to intrude.

SARAH

(confused)
I'll do whatever you wish, Sir William.

SIR WILLIAM

Good. Good. Well then, we'll have supper now, my dear.

INT. DINING ROOM - EVENING

Sir William, Lady Betty and Sarah are at the dining table. Sarah looks tentatively at Sir William, who eats silently, engrossed in his own thoughts. He suddenly addresses her.

SIR WILLIAM

What schooling have you had, Sarah?

SARAH

Why none, sir, save what I learned about the house. I can read, and I write a little.

LADY BETTY

Surely, William, conversation about schooling is premature. Sarah has only just arrived.

SIR WILLIAM

But education is important. Don't you agree, my dear?

LADY BETTY

Of course, William. But Sarah needs an opportunity to settle in. To get to know us, and we her.

SIR WILLIAM

She must be educated if she's to live in this house. But no rush. I'll look into it.

Lady Betty picks up a plate of food and offers it to a now frightened Sarah, who shakes her head to indicate no. Sir William looks up and reprimands her.

SIR WILLIAM

Speak up, Sarah. Speak up! We observe the best of manners in this house.

SARAH

(fearfully)

No, thank you, Lady Betty. I've had quite enough.

They continue to eat silently.

INT. LADY BETTY'S BEDROOM - NIGHT

Lady Betty and Sir William are in heated conversation.

LADY BETTY

You promised to be charitable and give her time! You know how tragic her life has been.

SIR WILLIAM

Her poor beginning is no concern of mine! I've raised one daughter and have little patience to raise a second. I gave you warning.

INT. DRAWING ROOM/WOODSTOCK - DAY

Lady Betty and Sarah are reading together when Sir William, looking self satisfied, enters and sits.

SIR WILLIAM

I've concluded my inquiries about schooling, and confirmed the reputation of Miss Parke's in Kilkenny. Sarah shall begin her studies on Friday fortnight.

LADY BETTY

But Kilkenny is so far away, William! And the family is arriving then. I won't be able to go with her.

SIR WILLIAM

My point exactly! You'll have enough to see to without attending to Sarah. Kilkenny isn't a long journey. She came here alone, she can go there alone. You wish to be educated don't you, Sarah?

SARAH

If you wish it, Sir William.

SIR WILLIAM

There. You see, my dear. Sarah is pleased to go to school. You needn't worry on her account.

Lady Betty and Sarah look distressed, but do not reply.

EXT. WOODSTOCK - DAY

A coach draws to a stop to collect Sarah and her few belongings. Lady Betty cries softly and dabs at her eyes with a handkerchief. Sarah looks emotionlessly around.

LADY BETTY
> Don't be sad, Sarah dear. I promise to visit within the month. The time will pass quickly, you'll see.

Sarah curtsies inappropriately and enters the coach.

INT. COACH - DAY

Sarah cowers in a corner and looks down at her clasped hands. Lady Betty nods to acknowledge the only other occupant, ELEANOR BUTLER, a mature 19, who watches the leave-taking with interest. As the coach moves off Eleanor looks silently at Sarah, then finally addresses her.

ELEANOR
> Sometimes painful events reveal themselves over time to be blessings in disguise. I know this to be a fact.

Sarah looks up to see a softly smiling Eleanor looking intently at her.

ELEANOR
> My name is Eleanor Butler. Since we're destined to travel together for a time, perhaps I could know your name.

SARAH
> Sarah Ponsonby.

ELEANOR
> So, Sarah Ponsonby, where are you going that frightens you so?

SARAH
> I'm not afraid. I don't feel anything.

Eleanor quietly absorbs this response before speaking again.

ELEANOR
> Not even sadness at leaving home?

SARAH

I *have* no home. I was supposed to live with my
dear cousin, Lady Betty, but I've been sent away by
Sir William.

ELEANOR

And where is "away?"

SARAH

To Miss Parke's in Kilkenny.

ELEANOR

Ah! Then I think you're a very lucky young lady. It's
a fine school. Don't you wish to learn?

SARAH

Oh yes, indeed I do! Books have been my only
friends. Some I have read many, many times. They
have sustained me.

ELEANOR

Sustained you? But you're so young. What has your
life been like to describe it so?

*Sarah tries to respond but starts to cry instead. Eleanor,
alarmed, moves to sit beside her and hands her a handkerchief.*

ELEANOR

There, there. Sometimes it's good to cry. When you
feel a little better you can tell me everything about
yourself.

LATER

Sarah is now more composed and talks quietly but intently.

SARAH

And so my dear cousin agreed to take me... But God
is punishing me, and I'm being sent away again!

ELEANOR

I do not believe in a punishing God.

SARAH

But I've prayed to Him! And I do naught but good,
yet I'm sent away.

ELEANOR

God sends us many trials to test us and build our strengths. Your early years were most unfortunate, Sarah. But look how strong you are, and see how your fortunes have changed. A beautiful new home, a cousin who loves you very much, and an opportunity to learn. You must keep these positive things foremost in your thoughts.

SARAH

Do you know Miss Parke's school?

ELEANOR

I know it well. I've never seen an unhappy student there... I was just 13 myself when I was sent away to school.

SARAH

Didn't you miss your home?

ELEANOR

(musing, remembering)
I did. Far more than I expected.

SARAH

How did you manage?

ELEANOR

I was sent to a convent. The Sisters were very kind, and a distant cousin lived not too far away. A gracious lady who made her home mine... Have you no acquaintances in Kilkenny?

SARAH

None at all.

ELEANOR

That *is* unfortunate.

Eleanor becomes thoughtful, then looks out the coach window.

ELEANOR

Good heavens. We've arrived already. How quickly the time has passed.

EXT. PARKE SCHOOL - DAY

*A cottage with a sign PARKE SCHOOL FOR GIRLS.
Eleanor disembarks first, and turns to help Sarah out. The
door of the school opens and BEATRICE PARKE, a strikingly
beautiful woman in her mid 20's, exits, comes to Eleanor and
hugs her.*

BEATRICE

Eleanor, what a surprise. You're back early.

ELEANOR

Hello, Beatrice. Yes, my budget too rapidly exhausted
by the temptations of the city.

BEATRICE

True to form. And?

ELEANOR

I've found every book you wanted. I'll send them over
as soon as I unpack.

BEATRICE

Lovely. Thank you, Eleanor.

ELEANOR

Let me introduce your new pupil, Miss Ponsonby.
Sarah, this is my friend, Miss Parke, who will be your
teacher.

BEATRICE

Welcome to Parke School, Sarah. I didn't know you
were acquainted, Eleanor.

ELEANOR

Sarah and I are acquainted only by chance. We met
on the coach.

BEATRICE

How fortunate. Well, Sarah, you'll want to say good-
bye to Lady Eleanor. Come along in when you're
ready. Shall I see you Sunday, Eleanor?

ELEANOR

Without fail. The risk to my faculties without the
stimulation of your conversation is not to be borne.

Beatrice laughs, picks up Sarah's suitcase and reenters the school.

SARAH

You are *Lady* Eleanor. Why didn't you tell me?

ELEANOR

Titles are sometimes an inconvenience, Sarah. To you I wish always to be Eleanor.

SARAH

Then I can see you again?

ELEANOR

(surprised)
If that would please you, of course you may.

SARAH

When, Eleanor? When?

ELEANOR

Let me think... Wednesdays are school half-days. I'll come on Wednesday and you can tell me how you're doing.

SARAH

Oh, thank you, Eleanor. Thank you.

Sarah hugs Eleanor impulsively, then turns to enter the school as Eleanor thoughtfully reenters the coach.

EXT. RIVER FOOTPATH - DAY

Sarah talks excitedly to Eleanor as they walk near the Nore River in Kilkenny.

SARAH

Oh, Eleanor, it's just as you said. I'm so happy.

ELEANOR

And I'm happy for you. Now tell me about your studies.

SARAH

I'm improving my handwriting. And I'm learning arithmetic, very good at it in fact. Next week I'm to start embroidery.

At the mention of embroidery Eleanor rolls her eyes, but is distracted by the SOUND OF A LARK.

ELEANOR

A lark! Listen... Do you know the songs of birds, Sarah?

SARAH

I've never much thought of birds.

ELEANOR

Oh, but you *must*. God's simplest creatures are His finest. They have no prejudices, they do not scheme, malice is unknown to them... I'll teach you to hear them. Now, about your studies. You learn no languages?

SARAH

No. We don't study languages.

ELEANOR

I have an offer to make. Would you like to learn French? I'm quite expert in it. I've always fancied myself a tutor, and I'd be pleased to teach you.

SARAH

Oh, yes! I'd love it, Eleanor.

ELEANOR

Then we'll start this very moment... Vocabulary first, I think. Yes. In French all objects are either feminine or masculine. So there are two forms for the word "the." If an object is feminine it is "la," and if it is masculine it is "le."

Sarah pays attention, but looks confused.

ELEANOR

It will seem confusing at first. That's to be expected, but it's really not difficult. For example "the dress," as you might expect, is feminine. Therefore it is "la robe." "The shoe," on the other hand, is masculine, it is "le soulier."

SARAH

(pronouncing perfectly)
La robe, le soulier.

ELEANOR

You have an excellent ear. Oh, this will be most enjoyable, Sarah!

They continue along the river. Eleanor identifies objects, Sarah repeats after her.

INT. DRAWING ROOM/CASTLE -AFTERNOON

Lady Betty and Sarah are being entertained by Lady Butler and Eleanor. Sarah sits tightly pressed against Eleanor, who has her arm around her. There are many additional ugly portraits hanging on the walls in the otherwise unchanged room. Lady Butler is arranging cups on a tea tray which sits in front of her.

LADY BETTY
It's such a pleasure to meet you, Lady Butler. Sarah has told me so much about Lady Eleanor's kindness to her. And, of course, your own.

LADY BUTLER
Sarah is a delight. And how are your lessons going, Sarah?

SARAH
Very well, Lady Butler. Especially my French lessons with Eleanor.

LADY BUTLER
(incredulous)
Your French lessons with Eleanor?

ELEANOR
I've been teaching Sarah French. Very enjoyable for both of us.

LADY BUTLER
Very commendable, Eleanor. I'm delighted with your new pursuit.

Lady Butler notices Lady Betty looking at one of the portraits.

LADY BUTLER
Have you an interest in portraits, Lady Betty?

LADY BETTY
I do.

LADY BUTLER
Then you'll be surprised to learn that these were done by this very hand.

She indicates her hand

LADY BUTLER
You may particularly notice the backgrounds. I use color to express each character... What do you think?

Lady Betty looks politely at the portraits.

LADY BETTY

Very effective.

LADY BUTLER

Thank you.   It's flattering to have one's work admired.

Lady Butler notices Sarah looking around the room.

LADY BUTLER

You haven't seen this room before, Sarah? Please feel free to look around.

Sarah smiles and walks directly to a large needlepoint on a standing frame. Eleanor walks to stand beside her as Lady Butler begins to pour tea.

SARAH

How beautiful.

LADY BUTLER

Do you like to needlepoint, Sarah?

SARAH

I'm learning embroidery, but I haven't done needlepoint.

ELEANOR

The pursuit of idle hands and empty heads.

SARAH

How so, Eleanor? My head isn't empty when I do embroidery. It's filled with dreams, and plans, and happy thoughts. I very much enjoy it just for itself.

LADY BUTLER

Well spoken, Sarah! My sentiments exactly.

SARAH

Is it very difficult?

ELEANOR

Not in the least. I'll be happy to show you how it's done.

LADY BUTLER

But you don't needlepoint, Eleanor!

ELEANOR

Disinclination doesn't signify inadequacy. I'm competent. If Sarah wishes to learn I'll teach her.

LADY BUTLER
You're full of surprises today, Eleanor.
(to Lady Betty)
I've never seen Eleanor so obliging. Having Sarah as a friend has been remarkably good for her.

EXT. CASTLE GARDEN - DAY

The previously neglected garden is now bursting with color. Lady Butler is showing it off to Lady Betty.

LADY BUTLER
What do you think? Isn't it glorious?

LADY BETTY
Beyond description! Your gardener is to be commended.

LADY BUTLER
Oh, but we've designed it ourselves... Of course Eleanor is a particular help. She's most knowledgeable about plants.

Eleanor's face registers amusement at Lady Butler's taking credit for the garden. She's surprised when Lady Betty smiles knowingly at her.

LADY BETTY
We must be getting along. A delightful day, Lady Butler, Lady Eleanor. Thank you most sincerely for your kind welcome.

ELEANOR
Don't forget your lesson on Wednesday, Sarah.

Sarah hugs Eleanor and leaves with Lady Betty.

INT. CASTLE/LIBRARY - DAY

Sarah is haltingly reading French verbs while Eleanor from time to time corrects her minor mispronunciations.

ELEANOR
Enough for today, Sarah. You're doing remarkably well.

Sarah smiles with pleasure.

ELEANOR
Unfortunately we must miss a lesson next week.

SARAH

Are you going away?

ELEANOR

No, on the contrary, someone is coming to see me.
An eminent suitor from Waterford.

SARAH

A suitor? But Waterford is so far away! I'll never
see you.

ELEANOR

Ah. You assume I'll accept his offer. I can assure you
I won't.

SARAH

Why do you see him if you don't care for him?

ELEANOR

I've never met him, so I don't know if I'll care for
him or not. In any event, I'm not prepared to marry
him.

SARAH

I don't understand. If you decide you like him why
won't you marry him? You've said he's eminent.

ELEANOR

Marriage is not for everyone, Sarah.

SARAH

But everyone must marry! It's understood.

ELEANOR

It's misunderstood. Everyone should *not* marry.
I, especially, should not.

SARAH

If you feel this way why do you see him at all?

ELEANOR

How persistent you are, Sarah!

SARAH

You haven't answered my question, Eleanor. Why do
you see him if you are determined not to marry him?

ELEANOR

(shaking her head in resignation)
Since you must know, I do it to keep the peace.
As long as it appears I'm interested in matrimony,
I placate my mother, whose passion it is to see me
successfully married.

SARAH

It all seems quite deceptive.

ELEANOR

It *is* deceptive, but necessary. And now *you* must be deceptive, too. These are very private thoughts I share with you, Sarah.

SARAH

(very seriously)

I'll say nothing, Eleanor. You know I won't.

ELEANOR

A reminder doesn't go astray on such an important issue... I do my parents a favor to remain unwed. They don't appreciate, but will in their declining years, the comfort of my presence and care. Not the role I would have chosen, but in the circumstances the better of the choices open to me.

SARAH

Let's have our lesson outside next time if the weather allows.

ELEANOR

An excellent idea. Now, off you go. Don't forget the roses for Beatrice.

Eleanor picks up a beautiful bouquet of deep red roses, which Sarah takes from her in gentle awe.

SARAH

They look like velvet.

ELEANOR

(surprised)

That's exactly what I see in them. And here's a special rose just for you.

She hands Sarah a perfect white rose.

SARAH

Oh, Eleanor! You're so good to me.

INT. DRAWING ROOM/CASTLE - EVENING

Lord Walter and Lady Butler are dressed for dinner.

LADY BUTLER
Well, Walter, we must hope Eleanor finds this match acceptable.

LORD WALTER
Kevin is a fine man. I'm sure she'll recognize his virtues.

LADY BUTLER
Recognizing his virtues and accepting his offer are *not* synonymous. Let's pray for the latter.

INT. DINING ROOM/CASTLE - EVENING

Lady Butler is at one end of an elaborately laid out table, Lord Walter at the other. Eleanor and MR. KEVIN DELANEY, a handsome man in his mid 50s, sit on opposite sides. Eleanor looks moderately disinterested, but polite.

LADY BUTLER
Mr. Delaney is one of the most successful merchants in Waterford, Eleanor.

ELEANOR
(surprised)
I understood you were retired, Mr. Delaney.

MR. DELANEY
To be sure I am, Lady Eleanor. I enjoy my ease.

ELEANOR
And what do you do to amuse yourself in your retirement?

MR. DELANEY
As little as possible, else it would not be retirement, would it? Ha, ha.

ELEANOR
Don't you travel now you have the time?

MR. DELANEY
I have no interest in travel.

ELEANOR
Then you read, perhaps?

MR. DELANEY
Very seldom. I find books tiresome.

Lord Walter interrupts in an effort to diffuse what is becoming a rapid interrogation by Eleanor of an increasingly nervous Mr. Delaney.

LORD WALTER
I'm not much of a reader myself, Kevin.

Eleanor ignores her father.

ELEANOR
Then no doubt you have an interest in politics?

MR. DELANEY
None at all.

ELEANOR
Then walks. Perhaps you walk?

MR. DELANEY
(relieved)
Yes! Yes, I do walk. I enjoy watching the waterfront. The packets sail daily to Wales you see, and there's much interesting activity. The quay is near my home.

ELEANOR
Near your home?

MR. DELANEY
(proudly)
Barely a hundred yards away. A very pleasant stroll.

ELEANOR
But how else do you pass your time? You must do something to fill it.

MR. DELANEY
Not at all. Time passes quite pleasantly. I repose myself. I enjoy my pipe. And my dogs. I do enjoy my dogs.

ELEANOR
And they you, no doubt. Yes, I expect you are like company.

Mr. Delaney looks confused. Lady Butler is outraged and quickly interjects.

LADY BUTLER
Dogs are great companions, Mr. Delaney. Eleanor is also very fond of dogs. Aren't you, Eleanor?

ELEANOR

Indeed, I am. Faithful beasts. A great comfort.

All lapse into silence as dinner is served.

INT. FOYER/CASTLE - EVENING

Lord and Lady Butler and Eleanor are saying good-bye to Mr. Delaney.

ELEANOR

A safe journey home, Mr. Delaney.

As the door closes behind Mr. Delaney Lady Butler turns furiously on Eleanor.

LADY BUTLER

How *dare* you shame your father and me with such discourtesy! What came over you, Eleanor?

ELEANOR

(trying to sound contrite)
I don't know, mother. I'm very sorry, my behavior was unpardonable. He's a very nice man, just so dull. I promise I'll never be disrespectful again.

LADY BUTLER

(still furious, but slightly mollified by the apology)
I should hope not, or it will be impossible for me to arrange a match for you. Well, we may as well call it a night. What a useless evening!

Lady Butler turns disgustedly toward the stairs, Lord Walter and Eleanor following.

EXT. BENCH NEAR RIVER NORE - DAY

Eleanor closes a book to complete a lesson with Sarah.

ELEANOR

It's time for you to get back to school.

SARAH

When will I see you again, Eleanor?

ELEANOR

Sooner than you think. I have a surprise for you. I will henceforth see you each Sunday. In addition to Wednesdays, of course.

SARAH

(very excited)

Will you truly, Eleanor? But why?

ELEANOR

I've decided to attend church with you. You're too condemning of yourself, and I lay the blame to religion. I hope to change this.

SARAH

I'm so happy you'll come to services at last.

(very seriously)

I'd be happier still if you believed, Eleanor.

ELEANOR

Oh, I believe, Sarah. But true belief comes from inside, not out.

SARAH

I don't know what you mean.

ELEANOR

I know you don't, but some day you will. I have another reason for my decision. Frankly, I'm bored. It will be interesting to resume discourse on things biblical, there being so many contradictions in the written word.

INT. CHURCH - DAY

Eleanor and Sarah are sharing a hymnal and singing On Jordan's Bank.

CU: Eleanor's and Sarah's hands holding the hymnal.

DISSOLVE

SAME SCENE SIX YEARS LATER.

Pull back to reveal a 19 YEAR OLD SARAH and Eleanor, 25, finishing the identical hymn. They sit to listen to a sermon given by NIGEL DAVENPORT, a handsome young curate.

EXT. CHURCH - DAY

Eleanor and Sarah exit and are greeted by Nigel, who is shyly interested in Sarah.

ELEANOR

Another thoughtful sermon, Nigel.

NIGEL

Thank you, Lady Eleanor. Good day, Miss Ponsonby.

SARAH

Good day to you, Mr. Davenport.

NIGEL

You were missed last week.

SARAH

Why, thank you. I was obliged to be at Woodstock.
Very enjoyable, but I'm delighted to be back.

ELEANOR

(interrupting)

I have something you'll wish to read immediately,
Nigel. By a French author, Jean Jacques Rousseau. I
couldn't put it down. I brought you the original in
French as I found the translation flawed.

Nigel takes the small booklet Eleanor offers him.

NIGEL

And the subject is – –

ELEANOR

Original sin. Or lack of it, to be precise. That's all I'll
say of it. I don't want to spoil it for you. I anticipate
we'll have many interesting discussions on Monsieur
Rousseau's point of view.

NIGEL

And I'll perhaps be forced to concede or desist, the
topic having been chosen by yourself.

ELEANOR

Come, Nigel, can't you see your faith is strengthened
by my challenge of it?

NIGEL

That's the most redeeming feature of our argument,
Lady Eleanor. Save my opportunity to point out
scriptural accuracy.

ELEANOR

The words of men, Nigel, the words of men. And
very old, odd words at that. Out of context in this
modern age.

NIGEL

Now, now Lady Eleanor, a little respect. It *is* the Sabbath after all.

ELEANOR

Be content that I respect *you*, Nigel. Don't ask the impossible... You'll be coming for tea?

NIGEL

With pleasure. Will you also be there, Miss Ponsonby?

SARAH

Indeed I shall, Mr. Davenport. I look forward to a detailed report of your recent journey.

NIGEL

And I to telling you all about it. 'Til tea then.

SARAH

'Til tea.

Eleanor and Sarah turn and, arms entwined, walk in silence for several minutes.

ELEANOR

Nigel is quite taken with you, Sarah.

SARAH

Really, Eleanor! I'm a good listener, that's what he finds attractive.

ELEANOR

Yes, a good listener *is* attractive. Still, it seems more than that... Be careful you give him the message you intend. Nigel is a dear friend, and I wouldn't wish him wounded. He's slow to warm, but unshakable in commitment... What a pity he's a second son. His brilliance can't be offset by his dismal prospects.

SARAH

Are they so dismal, Eleanor? He'll no doubt rise in the church.

ELEANOR

Yes, he'll rise. But where is there to rise *to*? It's so limiting.

SARAH

Isn't serving God compensation enough? Had I been a man I'd have welcomed the opportunity.

ELEANOR

Sarah, Sarah! I forever marvel how differently we think. You so rooted in the Scriptures and so accepting of the ramblings of well intentioned, and not so well intentioned, preachers. Sometimes I think I've taught you nothing.

SARAH

You've taught me everything. But wouldn't you judge yourself a failure if I hadn't the independence of thought and spirit you so admire in others?

ELEANOR

Touché, Sarah. Touché.

SARAH

Do we have time for our walk before tea?

ELEANOR

Most assuredly. Tea may be foregone, walks may not. Some desires are not negotiable.

They begin to walk briskly hand in hand across a field toward a high knoll in the distance.

EXT. TOP OF KNOLL - DAY

Sarah stands with the sun behind her, clearly outlining her breasts and slender body beneath her dress. A gentle breeze blows her hair as Eleanor, seated, looks up and sees her silhouette. Eleanor's eyes fill briefly with undisguised love, but she controls herself as Sarah walks to sit beside her.

ELEANOR

So, tell me the latest from Woodstock.

SARAH

Nothing changes. More insistence that I return to take up my duties.

ELEANOR

Yes, it will come to that. You can't resist indefinitely.

SARAH

It's been difficult to persuade Sir William to let me stay this long. He so heartily disapproves of my being "in trade."

ELEANOR

    Teaching is hardly that, but he would... How I dread your leaving.

SARAH

    I can't bear to think of it. So let's not... Hadn't we better start back?

ELEANOR

    Yes, we mustn't be late.

INT. KILKENNY INN - EVENING

Nigel and Sarah enjoy a candlelight supper in a very elegantly appointed dining room. They are in animated conversation. Nigel's face glows, but Sarah, naively, doesn't seem aware that he's romantically interested. Eleanor enters with Lord Walter, and is startled to see them. Eleanor and Lord Walter stop to say hello. Sarah stands spontaneously and hugs Eleanor, whose response is stiff, puzzling her. Nigel stands to shake hands with Lord Walter.

LORD WALTER

    Good evening Nigel, Sarah.

NIGEL

    A good evening to you, sir. And to you, Lady Eleanor.

SARAH

    You're dining out this evening, Eleanor?

ELEANOR

    Mother's away, so we had a chance to escape. Don't let us interrupt you.

Eleanor and Sir Walter walk to a table out of view of Sarah and Nigel. Eleanor looks uncomfortable, and her father, unaware, comments as they pick up and study their menus.

LORD WALTER

    That would be a good match. Keep your friend nearby in the bargain... Well Eleanor, what shall it be?

Eleanor rivets her attention on the menu and does not comment.

EXT. FAIR - DAY

Sarah and Beatrice walk together through the crowd at a busy county fair.

BEATRICE
Did Eleanor say exactly where we should meet?

SARAH
Unfortunately not. We didn't anticipate such crowds... Wait! There she is.

Sarah raises her hand to attract Eleanor's attention just as SIR GEOFFREY BANNISTER, tall and handsome, now in his early 30's, approaches and takes her joyfully in his arms. They begin to talk animatedly. As Sarah and Beatrice tentatively approach, Sarah's face registers discomfort, Beatrice's intense interest. Geoffrey notices them first. Eleanor follows his gaze and sees them.

ELEANOR
Sarah, Beatrice! Come share in a happy, happy reunion. Let me introduce my dear friend, Sir Geoffrey Bannister, whom I've told you so much about. Geoffrey, Miss Beatrice Parke, and Miss Sarah Ponsonby.

GEOFFREY
Delighted. My lucky day, indeed. Three charming ladies to keep me company when I'd expected to be dismally alone.

ELEANOR
(shaking her head)
Still the charmer, Geoffrey.
(to Sarah and Beatrice)
Geoffrey's just returned from his obligatory continental tour. The only person of my acquaintance who would rather have stayed at home than seen the sights.

GEOFFREY
Guilty. Ireland is my love. I'm not myself when I'm not on her blessed soil... Beatrice Parke? Why don't I know this name?

BEATRICE

I'm Irish by choice, not birth, Sir Geoffrey. I grew up in Devon, so it's unlikely you'd have heard the name.

ELEANOR

Beatrice is the mistress of Parke School for Girls, Geoffrey. Sarah was her pupil, and is now a teacher there.

GEOFFREY

I'm very pleased to meet you, Miss Parke. And you, Miss Ponsonby. Well then, shall we take in the sights?

Geoffrey extends his arm to Eleanor and they begin to stroll. Sarah and Beatrice follow at a slight distance.

ELEANOR

I've heard your father isn't well, Geoffrey.

GEOFFREY

He's the reason for my return. He came down with a terrible cough and fever, and it persists, relentless. We fear consumption, of course.

ELEANOR

Dreadful. Such a wonderful man. I know the anguish you must feel.

GEOFFREY

It's the time I've wasted in stupid travel when I could have been here to assist him that most distresses me.

ELEANOR

You had no choice. Wasn't I witness to your parents' insistence that you go? The purse rules. We do as we are bid.

GEOFFREY

Yes, you were there. I thank you for the reminder... It isn't just father's illness. The estate needs new direction, it's too dependent on crops. I want to diversify into cattle. Come look at them with me, Eleanor. You're a good judge of stock.

INT. ANIMAL STALLS/FAIR - DAY

Geoffrey and Eleanor are in a stall examining a beautiful Hereford, while Sarah and Beatrice watch.

GEOFFREY

This is what I want to breed. Herefords. But I can't even raise the subject as father is dead against it.

ELEANOR

Try to be patient. I feel things always resolve themselves as they are meant to.

They resume their stroll and are briefly silent. Then Geoffrey looks over his shoulder at Beatrice and Sarah.

GEOFFREY

Your friend seems very nice.

ELEANOR

Sarah is the greatest joy in my life.

GEOFFREY

(embarrassed)
I meant Miss Parke.

ELEANOR

Beatrice? Beatrice is splendid. A self-made, independent woman. An enviable position.

GEOFFREY

She's very beautiful.

Eleanor stops walking and looks intently at Geoffrey.

ELEANOR

Well then, Geoffrey, I think it's appropriate that you determine for yourself how splendid Beatrice is. Especially as I'm overdue to give my friend some attention.

GEOFFREY

Thank you, Eleanor. I'm deserted, Miss Parke. Would you be kind enough to walk with me?

BEATRICE

Delighted, Sir Geoffrey.

Geoffrey and Beatrice begin to walk side by side conversing, as Eleanor and Sarah drop slightly behind.

GEOFFREY

You're a long way from Devon, Miss Parke. Why Kilkenny?

BEATRICE

Ireland captivated me. Quite a shock, I can assure you. I came only for a short visit.

GEOFFREY

And couldn't leave?

BEATRICE

Could not forget, and returned.

GEOFFREY

And you are a teacher?

BEATRICE

Somewhat more than that. I founded Parke School.

GEOFFREY

Ah! I thought perhaps your father – –

BEATRICE

A magistrate. A kind and wise man who didn't bind me to a useless life of coquetry.

GEOFFREY

Wise, indeed. And brave, to let you go.

Sarah walks quietly but uncomfortably beside Eleanor.

SARAH

Sir Geoffrey seems to hold you in very high regard.

ELEANOR

We were partners in the most marvelous schemes. I hadn't realized how much I'd missed him.

SARAH

And he you, it seems.

Eleanor realizes that Sarah is jealous, and speaks gently.

ELEANOR

Geoffrey and I share many memories. His claim on my heart is of love and loyalty for a cherished childhood friend.

Sarah continues to look uncomfortable as they lapse into silence, stopping occasionally to view activities at the fair.

EXT. STREET - DAY

Sarah and Eleanor walk together. Sarah carries a book under her arm. They meet unexpectedly with Nigel, who is delighted to see Sarah.

NIGEL
Sarah! Lady Eleanor. What a pleasant surprise.

ELEANOR
Hello, Nigel. Where are you hurrying at such an early hour?

NIGEL
A very ill parishioner, I'm sorry to say. Are you off for a lesson?

SARAH
Yes. Such a perfect day we'll study outside.

NIGEL
And the topic today is - -

ELEANOR
French. Our old friend Mr. Rousseau, in fact.

NIGEL
Not *Noble Savages* at this hour, surely?

Sarah laughs and shows Nigel the book she's carrying.

SARAH
La Novelle Héloïse. A very romantic story.

NIGEL
Much more suitable.
(to Sarah)
I very much enjoyed your company at the play last week, Sarah. We must do it again soon.

SARAH
I'd love to. It was very enjoyable.

NIGEL
Well, I mustn't keep you.

Nigel resumes walking but suddenly stops, turns slowly around, a confused look on his face. He watches as Eleanor and Sarah, talking and laughing together, cross a small bridge suffused in sunlight. Shaking his head, he continues.

EXT. MEADOW - DAY

Eleanor and Sarah walk to sit under a large tree. The SONG OF A CURLEW is heard. Sarah listens intently.

SARAH
What a persistent little curlew.

ELEANOR
He surely is... What play did you and Nigel see?

SARAH
School for Scandal. Have you seen it? It was very funny.

ELEANOR
You didn't find the destruction of reputations by gossip and innuendo just a little thought provoking?

SARAH
It was just a comedy, Eleanor. Not to be taken seriously.

ELEANOR
Yet surely that was Mr. Sheridan's intent when he wrote it.

SARAH
(stubbornly)
That's not how I saw it.

ELEANOR
(testily)
And how do you see Nigel? Are you taking his interest seriously yet?

SARAH
We're just friends, Eleanor. In no way has Nigel indicated otherwise, and I do nothing to encourage him. Please let's not argue on such a magnificent day. We have so few of them together.

ELEANOR
Depressingly few.

SARAH
(opening the book)
Why don't I start with your favorite, Monsieur Saint-Preux's description of Héloïse and Claire's loving friendship?

ELEANOR

So like our own. Yes, start there.

Sarah smiles and thumbs through the novel. She reads aloud fluently in French.

SARAH

"J'étais jaloux d'une amitié si tendre. Rien sur la terre n'est capable d'exciter un si voluptueux attendrissement que – –"

As Eleanor watches Sarah, her eyes reveal her deep and pained love. Suddenly she reaches across to cover the book with her hand. Sarah, surprised, looks up.

ELEANOR

"Nothing on earth is capable of evoking such pleasure as so mutual an affection; the sight of two lovers could not have moved me more." Your French is perfect, Sarah. I'm restless today, let's walk a little further.

Eleanor gets quickly to her feet and brushes off her dress. She extends her hand to assist Sarah up, and they begin to walk slowly together.

INT. DRAWING ROOM/CASTLE - DAY

Lady Butler looks up from a letter as Eleanor enters.

ELEANOR

You sent for me, mother?

LADY BUTLER

I have some news that should please you, Eleanor. Geoffrey Bannister has petitioned your hand in marriage.

ELEANOR

Geoffrey? This *is* a surprise. He's been more often distracted and pressed for time than companionable these past months.

LADY BUTLER

I'm aware Lady Bannister has been pressing the issue since his father's death. I expect you to seriously consider Geoffrey. I'm growing weary of your rejection of perfectly acceptable suitors. Would Tuesday suit? I thought supper.

ELEANOR

Tuesday will be splendid.

LADY BUTLER

Don't be rude, Eleanor.

ELEANOR

I assure you I'm not being. I very much look forward to Geoffrey's visit.

INT. DINING ROOM/CASTLE - EVENING

A nervous Geoffrey and a very correct Eleanor are completing supper with Lord and Lady Butler.

LADY BUTLER

Well, Geoffrey, I expect you and Eleanor wish to be alone.

GEOFFREY

Thank you, Lady Butler. Lord Walter.

Lord Walter rises as they leave, then sits again.

LADY BUTLER

That seemed to go well. It will be a relief to have Eleanor settled. What a trial she's been to match.

LORD WALTER

She must take time and be happy in her choice.

LADY BUTLER

Don't talk nonsense, Walter! Marriage has nothing to do with happiness. It's security we're negotiating, not happiness. Small wonder Eleanor has such ridiculous notions about matrimony when her own father gives credence to them.

INT. DRAWING ROOM/CASTLE - EVENING

Eleanor and Geoffrey enter and close the door. Eleanor is very comfortable but Geoffrey looks nervous and wasted. They sit facing each other, and Geoffrey takes Eleanor's hands in his.

GEOFFREY

I apologize for not raising the subject of marriage on one of my previous visits, Eleanor.

ELEANOR

I think your timing is quite appropriate. No need to apologize.

Geoffrey's nervousness is replaced by a flattened, depressed mood. He speaks dispassionately.

GEOFFREY

Well, then. You're fully aware of my estate and the life I can offer you. We've always been such good companions. I truly feel we can make a life together. What do you think?

ELEANOR

I'm in complete agreement, Geoffrey. We can make quite an acceptable life together if we're so inclined. But I think you should know that I hold rather unconventional views in respect to marriage.

GEOFFREY

What views?

ELEANOR

I feel love to be an essential element, and while I know you love me, it's as a precious friend. A love not to be discounted, to be sure, but not the same as I refer to.

GEOFFREY

I think we could learn to love more deeply with time.

ELEANOR

Yes, I think we might...

Eleanor stands and walks slightly away from Geoffrey.

ELEANOR

But should we? The truth is, Geoffrey, I'm aware your affections lie elsewhere.

GEOFFREY

(shocked)

How could you know? I've said nothing.

ELEANOR

Dearest Geoffrey. Those who know love are most sensitive to it in others. Words aren't necessary.

GEOFFREY

Don't let that be a factor in your decision. It's finished.

ELEANOR

Beatrice has refused you?

GEOFFREY

I haven't asked her.

ELEANOR

Why not? You love her. She loves you.

GEOFFREY

Beatrice has no rank, no estate. Mother will never approve.

ELEANOR

Your mother doesn't have to approve. The estate is entirely yours since your father's death. Your mother is now living in your home, not you in hers.

GEOFFREY

That isn't quite true, Eleanor. If my choice doesn't conform mother would be impossibly disagreeable. I can't ask Beatrice to share such a life. She deserves better.

ELEANOR

If Lady Bannister chooses to be disagreeable build her a house of her own. Or a new one for yourself. You can well afford it.

GEOFFREY

You oversimplify the situation.

ELEANOR

I don't. What's the use of trying to please others? What suffices one day is anathema the next. Be true to yourself, Geoffrey, and all will go well... Aren't you at least willing to consider an alternative that can bring you so much joy?

Geoffrey lowers his head to his hands, shaken.

GEOFFREY

But what of my proposal to you?

ELEANOR

That's no impediment. I refuse you.

GEOFFREY

What will you tell your parents?

ELEANOR

The truth. That I refused you because you love Beatrice. Mother doesn't understand love. She'll be very angry. However, she must deal with that as she may.

Eleanor turns away and her eyes fill with tears.

ELEANOR

You're a man unequaled in my acquaintance, Geoffrey. Your friendship has brought me nothing but joy. But now *I* need a friend. My heart is so heavy, and I'm alone with its pain. I can't bear it any longer.

Geoffrey walks quickly to take Eleanor in his arms.

GEOFFREY

What is it, Eleanor? Of course I'm your friend. Have ever been, will ever be. You can tell me anything.

ELEANOR

I'm afraid the telling, hard as that may be, will surpass even your understanding.

GEOFFREY

Try me. If I can give back to you hundredfold what you've just given me it won't suffice. Tell me what's causing you such anguish?

ELEANOR

(hesitates, unsure)

As you feel for Beatrice, so I feel for Sarah. Love, for me, has chosen to break with tradition.

Geoffrey slowly comprehends, and totally accepts.

GEOFFREY

I never suspected your affection was of this nature.

ELEANOR

(breaks away from Geoffrey)

How could you? I'm expert at hiding it. Even from her. Sarah doesn't know how I feel. She's committed to family obligations and separation is inevitable. But suddenly I find myself wallowing in that same self-pity I so despise in others. I need to know that someone understands, and in duress, will care.

GEOFFREY

Then be assured I am that person, Eleanor. I agonize that I can't do for you what you've just done for me, and take your pain away. But hear me now when I tell you that I'll be for you always what you have been and are for me, the most treasured friend of my life. I love you, Eleanor, and nothing you ever do will change that.

EXT. CASTLE GARDEN - DAY

Eleanor stands near a bed of roses holding a small artist's paintbrush. Sarah excitedly approaches.

ELEANOR

Sarah. What brings you here? Not trouble I hope.

SARAH

Wonderful news! Lady Betty's dear friend, Mrs. Goddard, has sent an invitation which includes us. To attend the opera in Dublin. Will you come?

ELEANOR

Of course I'll come. When is this to be?

SARAH

A few weeks hence. My cousin will send the exact
dates. I can't believe it! To actually travel together, to
see all through each other's eyes. To share everything.

ELEANOR

It will be wonderful.

*Sarah is enraptured with anticipation for a few moments, then
notices the paintbrush in Eleanor's hand.*

SARAH

Are you taking up painting?

ELEANOR

(laughing)

Not on your life. There's nothing mother hates worse
than competition. No, I'm experimenting with cross
pollination.

SARAH

What's cross pollination?

ELEANOR

A technique King Louis' gardeners have developed. It
produces roses which never existed before.

SARAH

How extraordinary. Any luck?

ELEANOR

Not yet. The article I happened on had so few details
I find myself reinventing the technique rather than
duplicating it. Do you have time for tea before you
go?

SARAH

Yes. Luckily I do.

ELEANOR.

Then I'm triply blessed. You've come unexpected;
we'll go together to Dublin; and you'll stay for tea.
What matter no new rose. This day has brought far
greater rewards.

They walk arm and arm toward the Castle, talking excitedly.

INT. OPERA HOUSE - EVENING

*It's a gala event. Lady Betty, MRS. GODDARD, Sarah and
Eleanor make their way through the crowds and are seated.*

SARAH
It's so grand. Everyone looks so beautiful.

ELEANOR
Remember what I've told you.

SARAH
I will, Eleanor, I will.

*The lights dim, and the overture of a score by Glück (Iphigénie
en Aulide or Iphigénie en Tauride) begins. Short segments of
the opera are shown, building up to a lovely duet sung by a
soprano and tenor. Sarah's face becomes enraptured, and she
unconsciously reaches for Eleanor's hand. Eleanor shifts her eyes
to look briefly at their entwined fingers, covering them with her
free hand, then back at the stage, her eyes damp, until the duet is
complete, and the applause begins.*

INT. BEDROOM - NIGHT

*Sarah and Eleanor are in nightgowns. Eleanor is standing
brushing her hair, while Sarah wanders ecstatically with her
hands clasped in front of her breasts.*

SARAH
But the voices, Eleanor. They were angelic. Now I
see why you love it so. And I really do believe, as
you warned me, that it's best not to try to understand
every word. Of course I forgot, and made the attempt
- -

ELEANOR
Then you remembered - -

SARAH
and heard the voices... I hear them still.

Sarah stops and listens, as the DUET IS SUNG in background.

SARAH
Can you hear it, Eleanor? That wonderful duet?

Sarah begins to dance alone, a look of ecstasy spreading across her face, as Eleanor pauses to watch her.

SARAH

Dance with me, Eleanor.

They begin to dance together. Sarah smiles benignly at Eleanor, then, closing her eyes, moves to hold Eleanor closer. Her hand rises to draw Eleanor's head close to her own, then, without thinking she brushes her lips across Eleanor's cheek and kisses her briefly on the lips. Sarah's eyes slowly open to reveal a searching, confused, rising passion and she kisses Eleanor again deeply on the lips. Eleanor instinctively responds until Sarah, trembling uncontrollably, breaks away, looking at Eleanor in anguish.

SARAH

Oh, dear God! What have I done! Oh, Eleanor, forgive me! Forgive me! What's come over me? How could I do such a thing?

Sarah begins to cry.

ELEANOR

There's nothing to forgive! You've done nothing wrong.

SARAH

How can you say that! Oh, dear God! I'm possessed; I'm evil!

ELEANOR

You aren't evil! If I accept that *you* are evil, I must accept that I am also!

SARAH

What are you saying?

ELEANOR

That I feel as you do. I've loved you this way for years.

SARAH

Like this? But such things must not happen.

ELEANOR

Such things *do* happen. It's not common, but it's not evil. This I know.

SARAH

> I don't believe you! Man must not lie with man, nor woman with woman. St. Paul himself has written this.

ELEANOR

> The writings of a troubled man, Sarah! Not a directive from God. One doesn't choose to feel this way. One is chosen.

SARAH

> It was the music. I was bewitched by the music. This is never to happen again! If we are to remain friends we must be in complete agreement on this. Are we in agreement, Eleanor?

ELEANOR

> We are in agreement. Calm yourself, Sarah, we've injured no one. Calm yourself.

INT. DRAWING ROOM/CASTLE - DAY

Lady Butler works on a portrait of an androgynous looking individual wearing armor. Eleanor enters and stops to look at it.

LADY BUTLER

> Do you recognize her, Eleanor?

ELEANOR

> No. In fact I didn't realize it was a woman.

LADY BUTLER

> Then I've captured her perfectly! This is your greatest ancestress. Lady Penelope Brundage. What a warrior she was! Dressed as a man, and fought as one when security demanded it. Yes, indeed, we have a Joan of Arc in our very own family.

Eleanor points to a large brown blob on the left of the canvas.

ELEANOR

> What is this area meant to signify? It's not your usual.

LADY BUTLER

> The road of the warrior! Isn't it clever?

ELEANOR

(thinks for a minute, sighs)

I think it could use some perspective.

LADY BUTLER

What do you mean, perspective?

ELEANOR

(illustrates on the canvas)

If the road is wider here, then narrows here, it will give a greater sense of distance.

LADY BUTLER

Hum... No, too weak.

ELEANOR

Just a suggestion, mother. You are the artist, not I.

Eleanor wanders to a far window and parts the curtains to gaze out as Lady Butler resumes painting.

LADY BUTLER

I haven't seen much of Sarah lately. Has she been ill?

ELEANOR

Walking out with Mr. Davenport, I'm led to understand.

LADY BUTLER

Well, this is news! Of course Nigel's prospects are limited, but she'll have a decent living. She can't expect much better. Not as she has no estate, nor even, I suspect, the hope of a decent dowry... Yes, she's done well. Nigel is a fine man.

ELEANOR

(near tears; begins to recite softly, but with great emotion)

A man? "He is more than a man, he is a God in my eyes, he who sits beside her, listening intimately to her sweet voice and laughter, which makes my own heart beat fast. If I meet her suddenly, I cannot speak. A thin flame runs beneath my skin, seeing nothing, hearing only my own ears drumming. I drip with sweat, and trembling shakes my body. At such times death is not far from me."

LADY BUTLER

What *are* you babbling about, Eleanor?

ELEANOR

Nothing, mother. Nothing. Just a Greek poem.

LADY BUTLER

Oh, Greek ... Odd names those Greeks have.

Eleanor suddenly sobs and walks quickly from the room. Lady Butler is startled, looks mystified, twice starts to put down her palette, finally sighs and does, then exits.

INT. ELEANOR'S BEDROOM - DAY

The previously drab bedroom has been transformed into a virtual art gallery/library. The carpets, drapes, and bedspread of a beautifully carved four poster double bed are bright and cheerful. One wall is entirely filled with stocked bookshelves, and some beautiful paintings hang on other walls. Eleanor sits on the side of her bed, semi-composed. A KNOCK is heard, and the door opens.

LADY BUTLER

May I come in, Eleanor?

ELEANOR

Of course, mother.

Eleanor gets quickly to her feet as Lady Butler enters. She looks with surprise around the room.

LADY BUTLER

Why this is quite pleasant, Eleanor... So many books... This is an interesting painting, quaint... Well.

Lady Butler walks to the bedside, picks up a book lying on Eleanor's bedside stand, and flips through its pages.

LADY BUTLER

What language is this, Eleanor?

ELEANOR

Italian.

LADY BUTLER

How did you learn to read Italian?

ELEANOR

Sarah and I taught ourselves.

LADY BUTLER

I don't like Italians. Your father and I were unfortunate enough to be lodged next to some of those people on one occasion. Most unpleasant. I'm surprised they write anything worth reading.

Lady Butler stands silently for a few more minutes looking around the room.

LADY BUTLER

Very pleasant. Very. I'll take my leave now. Thank you, Eleanor.

ELEANOR

Thank *you*, mother.

INT. CHURCH - DAY

Nigel is near the altar as Sarah enters, looking pale and distraught. He comes immediately to grasp her hands.

NIGEL

Sarah. Dearest Sarah. Are you well? I was quite concerned to leave you last evening. You seemed not at all yourself.

SARAH

I'm *quite* well, thank you, Nigel.

NIGEL

It's my fault. I shouldn't have pressed so earnestly for an early date. You must be the one to choose. There's Lady Betty's health to consider. I - -

SARAH

Nigel, I must speak honestly with you.

NIGEL

Of course, my love. I know something is troubling you. I'm glad you feel you can trust me.

SARAH

I can't marry you, Nigel. I know these words will hurt you, but there is no kind way to say them.

NIGEL

You mean we must delay, I understand – –

SARAH

That's *not* what I mean. Please listen to me, Nigel. I can't marry you.

NIGEL

It's common to feel nervous, Sarah. I, who perform God's holy ceremony, know this very well.

SARAH

You haven't heard me, Nigel! *I said I cannot marry you!*

Nigel finally gets the message and becomes testy.

NIGEL

But we're betrothed. You've told me you love me.

SARAH

(paces in frustration)
I *do* love you. I'll *always* love you. But it's not the same, it cannot be the same.

NIGEL

The same as what?

SARAH

The same as what I've felt.

NIGEL

What are you talking about?

SARAH

What I've felt, what I feel for Eleanor.

NIGEL

For Lady Eleanor? But a loving friendship is a blessing. It's another of God's great gifts.

SARAH

This is no gift from God, it's an evil obsession! She invades every moment of my waking hours. I grow weak and must sit when, unbidden, she enters my thoughts. The pain I feel when I see her but must stay apart is indescribable.

Nigel recoils, disbelieving.

NIGEL

Carnal desire? Are you telling me you feel carnal desire for Lady Eleanor?

SARAH

Yes, yes! That *is* what I'm telling you. I love you, Nigel, but it doesn't compare, and it won't suffice. It would be unfair for me to marry you. I would only make you miserable.

Nigel backs away from Sarah, shocked, then enraged. He begins to pace, his head in his hands.

NIGEL

In God's house! You've come into God's house to tell me of this abomination! Oh, my God, and I have loved you with all my heart. What does this say of me? Why have I been so cursed? Oh, my God, my God!

SARAH

(shocked at Nigel's reaction, attempts to comfort him)
I know these feelings are evil, Nigel. I didn't come to hurt you, but to spare you.

NIGEL

(pushes her away from him)
Spare me? You've defiled me! Get away from me!

SARAH

(becoming frightened)
I *am* going. That's why I've come. To say good-bye.

NIGEL

Go! Get out! Please God I'll never set eyes on you again!

Sarah, now terrified, runs out of the church, as Nigel collapses into a pew weeping, his head in his hands.

EXT. CASTLE GARDEN - DAY

Eleanor is in her gardening clothes holding pruning shears as Sarah approaches. Sarah's eyes are empty, her face registers defeat and exhaustion.

ELEANOR.

Sarah. An unexpected visit.

SARAH

I won't stay long, Eleanor. I wanted to say good-bye.

ELEANOR

You're going?

SARAH

Yes. Today.

ELEANOR

I'm sorry to hear that. And Nigel?

SARAH

I've told him the truth.

ELEANOR

That was a brave thing to do. How did he take it?

SARAH

As you would expect. Horrified, enraged. My love has caused him so much pain... Oh, Eleanor, why us? What have we done to deserve such punishment?

ELEANOR

Don't think of it that way, Sarah. Many people experience not a moment of true love in their entire lives. At least we'll have that memory... You'll allow me to write won't you? And answer so that I'll know you're well?

SARAH

Yes, of course.

Sarah looks vacantly around the garden.

SARAH

Beautiful, as always. I've missed it. I shall miss it.

ELEANOR

I'm glad you came. I have something special for you.

Eleanor stoops, cuts a beautiful medium sized peach colored rose, and hands it to Sarah.

SARAH

So lovely. Thank you, Eleanor.

ELEANOR

You don't understand. This is my first new rose. I've named it the Sarah Ponsonby.

SARAH

The Sarah Ponsonby?

ELEANOR

It's customary to name a rose one develops. I've given it yours.

Sarah is stunned, tears spring to her eyes.

SARAH

It's so pure.

ELEANOR

As are you, Sarah. Pray God one day you'll see this.

SARAH

(shaken)

I must go. God bless you, Eleanor.

Sarah begins to sob, hugs Eleanor, then turns and walks rapidly away.

ELEANOR

God speed, my beloved.

Lord Walter has watched the interchange out of earshot. He walks quickly to Eleanor, who bursts into tears and throws her arms around him.

LORD WALTER

What is it, Eleanor? Sarah looked so distraught, and I find you in a like condition.

ELEANOR

Sarah is leaving Kilkenny.

LORD WALTER

But she's betrothed to Nigel.

ELEANOR

She's just told him she won't marry him. She's going back to Woodstock.

LORD WALTER

I'm so sorry, Eleanor. I know how much you'll miss her.

Eleanor is unable to conceal her anguished love, and turns quickly away. Lord Walter, recognizing it, is startled and confused. He puts his arm around Eleanor's shoulders, and holds her tightly as they walk slowly toward the Castle.

INT. ELEANOR'S BEDROOM - DAY

Eleanor sits at her desk writing a letter.

ELEANOR (VO)

> My dearest Sarah, It has been quite cold and dreary here today. A condition which matched my mood exactly, until your welcome letter arrived. It's a relief to hear you are well. I am also, as are my parents... Geoffrey has visited for the first time since the wedding and wishes to be remembered. I hope my warm reception dispelled the unpleasantness of mother's rudeness. In her opinion he may never be excused for what she considers his matrimonial deceit. Wonderful news. Beatrice is expecting. Geoffrey fair beamed with pride.

INT. SARAH'S BEDROOM/WOODSTOCK - DAY

Sarah, seated, reads Eleanor's letter. The now adult Frisk is at her feet, and she idly pets him.

ELEANOR (VO)

> Won't you reconsider if we may on occasion visit? I there, or you, here? I'll keep my promise, so why should we not meet as the loving friends we were for so many years? Let me say again how great is my anguish at not seeing you. I won't press the issue, but know that I live to one day share again, however briefly, some of our special moments, whose memories fill my days, and gently guide my dreams.

A KNOCK sounds at Sarah's bedroom door. As she looks up the door opens and Mary Carryl peeks in.

MARY CARRYL
> Pardon, Miss Sarah. Lady Betty is ready.

Sarah looks with alarm at a clock on her desk.

SARAH

Good heavens! I've kept her waiting.

Sarah rises, hastily picks up a shawl, and exits the room.

EXT. WOODED PATH - DAY

Sarah and an extremely frail Lady Betty, who leans heavily on Sarah and uses a cane, walk together. The day is overcast, with rain threatening.

SARAH

I think we should turn back. This is too difficult for you.

LADY BETTY

No, please Sarah, let's continue. I love this walk, and it's so rare I feel well enough to come this far. Don't deprive me.

SARAH

Dearest cousin, I'd deprive you of nothing. But I'm concerned you may overtax yourself.

LADY BETTY

I promise I won't exceed my limit... You're such a blessing to me, Sarah. It distresses me to see you so unhappy.

SARAH

I'm not unhappy, cousin. I'm where I most desire to be. At your side, to assist as I may.

LADY BETTY

But you're lonely. I sense this most acutely. You miss Eleanor very much, don't you?

SARAH

I do. We were for years such close companions. But I'll get over it.

LADY BETTY

Oh, you mustn't try to get over it! Friendship isn't rendered impossible by distance. Look at me, for example. I really don't know what I should have done without Mrs. Goddard. Sir William does his best, but men are so needy. Quite childlike really. One needs much support to cope, as you shall learn. Dear Mrs. Goddard has ever given it to me... Why even the Scriptures show us the example.

SARAH

The Scriptures?

LADY BETTY

In Ruth's devotion to Naomi, of course. You must know it. "Entreat me not to leave thee, nor return from following after thee. For wither thou goest I will go, and where thou lodgest – –"

SARAH

"I will lodge. Thy people shall be my people, and thy God my God. Where thou diest, will I die, and there will I be buried."

Sarah looks stunned, but recovers as THUNDER SOUNDS in the distance.

SARAH

I think we won't escape the storm. We'd best turn back.

LADY BETTY

It's still distant. Let's go just a little further. I'm pleased you remember the passage.

SARAH

(preoccupied)
I had forgot, I had forgot.

They walk on as the sky darkens above them. It begins to rain softly.

SARAH

Rain! No more objections. We must go back at once!

Lady Betty reluctantly follows Sarah's lead and they turn back. Within minutes they are caught in a deluge. The wind whips at their clothes, and they can barely move ahead.

EXT. WOODSTOCK - DAY

Mary Carryl watches from a window as Sarah and Lady Betty return. She runs out with fresh shawls and umbrellas, and helps Sarah to assist Lady Betty inside.

INT. LADY BETTY'S BEDROOM - DAY

MARY CARRYL

I'll take care of her ladyship, Miss Sarah. You must get out of those wet clothes.

LATER

A totally exhausted Lady Betty is in bed, being attended by Mary Carryl. Sarah enters and goes directly to the bedside.

SARAH

How are you, cousin?

LADY BETTY

Very comfortable, my dear. It was really quite thrilling. I loved to walk in storms when I was a girl. Did I ever tell you? It made mother quite angry.

SARAH

Rest now. I'll have dinner sent up, and stop in after I've seen to Sir William.

INT. DINING ROOM/WOODSTOCK - EVENING

Sir William is seated at the table looking quite impatient. Sarah enters hurriedly.

SIR WILLIAM

What kept you, Sarah? And where is Lady Betty?

SARAH

I'm sorry, Sir William. My cousin and I were caught in the storm. We were obliged to change as we were quite soaked. Lady Betty is dining in her room. She's somewhat tired from her outing.

SIR WILLIAM

She's always tired... It's good you're home, Sarah, else I should spend most of my time unattended.

SARAH

I'm pleased that I satisfy, Sir William.

Sir William looks searchingly at Sarah, his face unreadable. They lapse into silence as the meal is served.

INT. LADY BETTY'S BEDROOM - NIGHT

Mary Carryl stands by the bedside as Sarah enters wearing a nightgown covered by a shawl. Lady Betty has a damp cloth on her forehead.

SARAH
How is she, Mary?

MARY CARRYL
Resting at the moment, Miss Sarah. But she seems feverish, and is confused at times.

Lady Betty begins to groan feebly. She opens her eyes, slowly focuses on Sarah, weakly squeezes the hand Sarah offers her, then drifts again into unconsciousness. As Sarah replaces the damp cloth on Lady Betty's forehead Mary Carryl glances uneasily toward Sir William, who stands quietly in a corner. Sarah, following Mary Carryl's gaze, is badly startled to see him, and wraps her shawl protectively around her body.

SARAH
Sir William! I didn't see you.

SIR WILLIAM
No matter, my dear. I'm pleased you're so faithful in your duties. I won't disturb you.

As he exits he detours to pat Sarah on the shoulder. She watches as the door closes behind him, and shudders.

INT. STUDY/WOODSTOCK - DAY

Sir William stands gazing into the fire. Sarah enters.

SARAH
You sent for me, Sir William?

SIR WILLIAM
(half turns to address Sarah)
What's the latest from the sickroom?

SARAH
There's been little improvement. My cousin continues gravely ill.

SIR WILLIAM
She's been frail for many years. It seems very likely this may be the end. So we must talk of you, Sarah.

SARAH

Of *me*, Sir William? I don't understand.

SIR WILLIAM

(turns back to face the fire)

It's best that you know my desires, and have an opportunity to grow accustomed to them... I have no son to inherit the estate. I plan to remarry, in the hope I may yet have one.

Sarah's face registers shock, then disgust. Sir William is unaware of her reaction as he is still looking into the fire.

SIR WILLIAM

You've grown comely, Sarah. You suit me.

Sarah is horrified as she realizes Sir William means this to be a proposal. She manages to regain her composure as he turns and looks at her with barely disguised lust.

SARAH

I won't respond to this, Sir William. My cousin will recover. I beg you to excuse me so that I may attend her.

SIR WILLIAM

Go, go. But keep in mind my proposal. I'm sure you'll find it sensible.

Sarah turns and leaves with a look of genuine fear in her eyes.

INT. SARAH'S BEDROOM - DAY

Sarah writes at her desk, Frisk at her feet.

SARAH (VO)

My dearest Eleanor. A situation of the most desperate urgency has arisen.

INT. ELEANOR'S BEDROOM/KILKENNY CASTLE - DAY

A KNOCK SOUNDS on the door. Eleanor walks to answer it, and a maid, KATIE, presents a letter to her on a silver tray.

KATIE

An urgent letter, m'lady. And Lady Butler wishes to see you in the library at your convenience.

ELEANOR

Thank you, Katie. Tell her I'll be down directly.

Eleanor shuts the door, walks to her desk, picks up a letter opener, opens the letter, and sits to read it.

SARAH (VO)

My dearest Eleanor, a situation of the most desperate urgency has arisen. Lady Betty is gravely ill, and I am in great need of your counsel, which only your immediate presence can supply. I beg you to come at the earliest possible moment. In haste. Your devoted and loving friend, Sarah.

INT. LIBRARY/CASTLE - DAY

Lady Butler and Lord Walter are seated as Eleanor enters.

LADY BUTLER

Sit down, Eleanor. We want to discuss a possible new suitor. I've had great difficulty arranging this, but at last I think you'll approve my choice.

ELEANOR

(angrily)

I thought I had made it clear that I would not receive any more suitors, mother.

LADY BUTLER

You can't live here indefinitely, Eleanor. The estate will pass into other hands at your father's death.

ELEANOR

I'll deal with that when it happens. Discussion now is premature.

LADY BUTLER

(persisting)

The only alternative to marriage is the veil, and if this is your choice you must make it now while you are still young enough to be accepted.

ELEANOR

(disbelieving)

Become a nun! You can't be serious!

LADY BUTLER

It's the only way to ensure lifetime security. Your father and I are in total agreement on this point.

ELEANOR

(aghast)

Father?

LORD WALTER

(uncomfortable, unconvincing)

Your happiest days were at the convent. We thought – –

ELEANOR

My happiness there was as a child who delighted in learning. I have *no* interest in a cloistered life. To return is out of the question.

LADY BUTLER

If you are determined not to marry you *must* consider it, Eleanor.

Eleanor gives her mother a long penetrating stare. Then looks as if she has made a decision.

ELEANOR

As you say, mother, I must consider, and I shall do so. But for the moment it must wait. I've had an urgent letter from Sarah to report that Lady Betty is gravely ill, and she requests that I come at once. With your permission, I'll leave at dawn.

Lady Butler is surprised and relieved by Eleanor's apparent compliance.

LADY BUTLER

Go by all means! Perhaps Sarah can help you see the wisdom of our suggestion. Please give Lady Betty our wishes for a speedy recovery.

ELEANOR

Then if you'll excuse me, I'll prepare for my departure.

Eleanor turns and exits the room.

LADY BUTLER

Well, this is unexpected! Perhaps it won't be as difficult as we thought.

Lord Walter looks suspiciously at the closed door.

INT. ELEANOR'S BEDROOM - EVENING

The maid Katie packs a medium sized carpet bag.

ELEANOR
Pack my wool dress, Katie.

KATIE
It seems a bit heavy for April, m'lady.

ELEANOR
Pack it, and these.

Eleanor hands some silver boxes and a pretty desk clock to Katie, who looks surprised, but packs them without comment.

ELEANOR
Thank you, Katie. I'll finish myself.

Katie curtsies and leaves. Eleanor opens a locked desk drawer, takes out a considerable amount of money and some important looking papers, places these in the bag and locks it. A KNOCK SOUNDS, and the door is opened by Lord Walter.

LORD WALTER
May I come in, Eleanor?

ELEANOR
Of course, father.

Lord Walter is extremely uncomfortable. He looks penetratingly at Eleanor for several moments before speaking.

LORD WALTER
I'll respect your privacy, Eleanor, but I must know
your intentions.

ELEANOR
I won't return to this house, father.

LORD WALTER
You'd have left without telling me of your decision?

ELEANOR
I'd have written.

LORD WALTER
Surely we aren't reduced to that?

ELEANOR
I thought it best.

LORD WALTER

Where do you propose to go?

ELEANOR

To England... You know why I can never marry, father.

LORD WALTER

I don't want to talk about this, Eleanor.

ELEANOR

We must, because we may never meet again.

LORD WALTER

It's not natural, Eleanor – –

ELEANOR

It's not *usual*. It's perfectly natural for me.

LORD WALTER

Don't you care what people will say?

ELEANOR

I can't care. Do you propose that I let other people's opinions govern my life and conduct? What of *my* desires, *my* happiness? Have you no concern for me?

LORD WALTER

It's because I'm concerned that I take issue. I don't think you grasp the full implications.

ELEANOR

I grasp them in their entirety. I'm full aware of the difficulties.

LORD WALTER

I very much doubt you are, Eleanor... Your mother will be distraught.

ELEANOR

She doesn't want me here. I've determined on a plan to oblige her. She should be joyful.

LORD WALTER

She'll be disgraced when she learns of this affinity – –

ELEANOR

She need never know. Tell her anything you wish.

LORD WALTER

But Sarah – –

ELEANOR

Sarah isn't going with me. I stop only in response
to her appeal. When I've helped with Lady Betty I'll
go on alone.

LORD WALTER

(looks enormously relieved)
How do you propose to support yourself?

ELEANOR

With my annuity.

LORD WALTER

You can't live on that. Your tastes are expensive.

ELEANOR

Then I'll work. It's no concern of yours. You can't
stop me, father.

LORD WALTER

I won't stop you, Eleanor. You've given me so much
joy that I'll not interfere with a plan which you think
can bring you contentment... I'll send what I can.

ELEANOR

Thank you, father. I knew you'd understand.

LORD WALTER

I don't understand, Eleanor. I'll never understand.

*Lord Walter turns and exits with head bent, eyes full of
desolation. Eleanor sinks into a chair, her face registering a
mixture of exhaustion, relief, sadness.*

INT. SARAH'S BEDROOM - NIGHT

*An exhausted Sarah sits looking into an open fire. Frisk lies
beside her. A KNOCK sounds on the door.*

SARAH

Come in.

*The door opens and Sir William enters. Sarah, alarmed, stands
quickly.*

SARAH

Sir William! Has something happened to Lady Betty?

SIR WILLIAM

No, no! She remains the same. I thought this a good opportunity for us to visit. One needs solace at such a time.

SARAH

I appreciate your concern, Sir William, but I'm very tired. I was about to retire.

SIR WILLIAM

It takes little enough effort to talk, Sarah. We have much to discuss.

SARAH

I have nothing to say to you, Sir William.

SIR WILLIAM

It's quite appropriate that we be together. Lady Betty has been no wife to me these many years, and you and I shall soon be wed.

SARAH

I have not accepted your offer, Sir William. I must insist that you leave at once.

SIR WILLIAM

Now, now, Sarah. I can be gentle.

Sir William advances and attempts to take Sarah in his arms. Frisk barks loudly and jumps at Sir William as Sarah struggles to hold him off. They lose their balance and crash to the floor, Sir William is stunned as he hits his head in the fall. Sarah leaps to her feet and backs away from him. At that moment a QUICK KNOCK sounds on the door, which is opened by Mary Carryl, who enters immediately.

SARAH

Mary! Thank goodness you've stopped in. Sir William has had a spell in his grief over Lady Betty and may have injured himself. Please call Padraig to assist him to his room.

Mary Carryl walks quickly to a bell pull, then to Sir William. A servant, PADRAIG, enters, and together they get him to his feet, and from the room. Sarah turns a key in the lock, and leans against the door, looking ashen.

EXT. KILKENNY CASTLE - DAWN

Eleanor stands alone beside a coach as the driver loads her bag. He assists her inside, mounts and drives it away.

INT. WINDOW/CASTLE - DAWN

Lord Walter stands unseen by Eleanor, and watches her coach out of sight. He then walks to a chair and sits, buries his face in his hands, and cries softly.

INT. FOYER/WOODSTOCK - DAY

Eleanor enters just as Sarah rapidly descends the stairs. Before they can speak Sir William joins them from his study. Sarah looks exhausted, pale, and fearful.

SIR WILLIAM
> Well, Lady Eleanor. We thank you for coming so promptly.
> *(sarcastically)*
> Sarah is convinced you can teach the doctor his trade and perform a miraculous cure.

ELEANOR
> I'm happy to help in any way I can.
> *(to Sarah)*
> How is Lady Betty?

SARAH
> She continues gravely ill. Let me show you to your room, Eleanor. Then I'd be grateful if you'll see her for yourself. With your permission, Sir William?

Sir William nods assent, and after a penetrating look at Sarah turns back toward his study. Padraig enters with Eleanor's bag and follows them upstairs.

INT. GUEST BEDROOM - DAY

Padraig sets the bag down and quickly exits, shutting the door behind him. Sarah starts to cry and turns to Eleanor, who steps quickly forward to take her in her arms.

ELEANOR

> There, there. I'm here now to help. Tell me exactly how Lady Betty fares.

Sarah breaks away from Eleanor's arms and begins to pace aimlessly around the room. She's tense and distracted.

SARAH

> She's dying.

ELEANOR

> *(shocked, then alarmed)*
> There's something more, what is it?

Sarah stops and looks directly at Eleanor in great distress.

SARAH

> It's Sir William. He's made it plain he expects I'll welcome his attentions when my cousin dies.

ELEANOR

> Is he mad? This is - -

SARAH

> There's more. He's made an attempt. Dear God, it's so disgusting. I've got to get away, Eleanor. Is it possible? Will you help? Can you come with me?

ELEANOR

> Come with you? Are you sure this is what you want?

SARAH

> I *am*, truly I am, Eleanor. The feelings we have for each other can't be an accident. I'm no longer afraid. I accept.

Eleanor takes Sarah in her arms and holds her tightly for a few moments, as tears of joy and relief stream down her face.

ELEANOR

> I *do* have a plan, Sarah, but we'll need help. Let me explain.

INT. SARAH'S BEDROOM - DAY

Sarah is standing as A KNOCK sounds on the door.

SARAH

> Come in.

Mary Carryl enters.

SARAH

> Shut the door, Mary... Thank you... Please sit
> down...
> *(Sarah also sits, and takes Mary's hands in hers)*
> Mary, I need help of a very particular nature, and it
> requires the utmost discretion.

INT. LADY BETTY'S BEDROOM - LATE AFTERNOON

*Eleanor, Sarah and Mary Carryl are tending to the gravely ill
patient. As they turn her on her side Lady Betty briefly opens
her eyes, and slowly recognizes Eleanor. A peaceful smile lights
her face. She speaks weakly.*

LADY BETTY

> You've come. Now I may go, for I know you'll take
> care of her.

She drifts again into unconsciousness.

INT. GUEST BEDROOM - NIGHT

*A SOFT KNOCK sounds on the door. Eleanor wakes
immediately and gets out of bed, picks up and dons her robe, goes
to the door and opens it. Mary Carryl is standing outside.*

MARY CARRYL

> It's time. Please come, m'lady.

INT. LADY BETTY'S BEDROOM - NIGHT

*Sarah sits at the bedside of the dying Lady Betty, while Eleanor
and Mary Carryl stand behind her.*

MARY CARRYL

> Shall I rouse Sir William?

SARAH

> *(bitterly)*
> He doesn't deserve to be here.

*After a few distantly spaced breaths Lady Betty gives one last
soft expiration and dies. Eleanor holds Sarah as she begins to
cry softly.*

EXT. CEMETERY - DAY

A deeply grieving and anxious Sarah, a consoling Eleanor, and a self satisfied Sir William leave the cemetery in a chaise driven by Padraig.

EXT. WOODSTOCK - DAY

The chaise arrives and Sarah and Sir William disembark.

ELEANOR
I'm sorry I can't stay longer.

SIR WILLIAM
I'll take care of Sarah. Have no fear of that.

SARAH
Thank you for coming, Eleanor. A safe journey.

As they turn toward the house Sir William offers his arm to Sarah and, after a slight hesitation, she takes it. Eleanor anxiously watches them go.

INT. DINING ROOM/WOODSTOCK - EVENING

Sir William, who is eating robustly, and Sarah, who picks at her food, are at supper.

SARAH
We'll need to talk, Sir William. May I beg a delay until tomorrow. I'm exhausted, and would appreciate an early night.

SIR WILLIAM
Tomorrow will be perfectly satisfactory. All the time in the world now, my dear.

SARAH
Then with your permission – –

SIR WILLIAM
Go, go. Rest yourself until tomorrow.

Sarah rises and lays her napkin down, her face registering tension which lightens somewhat with relief as she exits.

EXT. HALLWAY OUTSIDE SARAH'S BEDROOM - NIGHT

Mary Carryl, a lowly lit lantern in her hand, KNOCKS on a bedroom door. It is immediately opened by Sarah, who is dressed in men's clothing, including a hat which completely covers her long hair. She hands Mary a traveling bag, and as she turns to shut the door Frisk rushes out. She stoops to pet him, and gently pushes him back into the room, closing the door. He starts to bark wildly, and Sarah, frightened, reopens the door and scoops him up. As he stops barking Sarah and Mary Carryl stand frozen, listening, but hear only silence. They turn toward a staircase at the rear of the house, and Mary leading, slowly descend to an outside door, where Padraig is waiting. He drapes a cloak over Sarah's shoulders, as she turns tearfully and hugs Mary Carryl.

SARAH
    I'll write, Mary.

MARY CARRYL
    God keep you safe, Miss Sarah.

Padraig takes Sarah's bag from Mary Carryl and assists her into a waiting coach. Eleanor is inside, also dressed in men's clothing and cloak. She takes Sarah's trembling hand in her own as Sarah sets Frisk down.

ELEANOR
    Frisk?

SARAH
    He barked uncontrollably.

ELEANOR
    Then he was meant to come.

The coach moves rapidly off, passing a sign reading
WATERFORD - 23 MILES

INT. SIR WILLIAM'S BEDROOM - EARLY DAWN

Sir William stretches, looks at the faint light of dawn, and sits on the side of his bed, suddenly animated.

SIR WILLIAM
    It's tomorrow!

He dons his robe, combs his hair, rinses his mouth, shaves, and splashes some cologne on his cheeks. He then looks at himself admiringly in a full length armoire mirror, nods with satisfaction, and heads for his bedroom door.

INT. SARAH'S BEDROOM - DAWN

The door is quietly opened by Sir William. It squeaks in several places, and at each squeak he stops and looks carefully toward the bed, where he can see the silhouette of a body. Once inside he closes the door as carefully as he has opened it, and tiptoes softly to the unoccupied side of the double bed. He slips off his robe, and begins to get into the bed, being careful to disturb the mattress as little as possible. When he is under the sheets he rests for a moment to catch his breath, then carefully turns and reaches for Sarah, looks puzzled, feels around, and as realization dawns, throws back the bed covers to reveal several pillows positioned to resemble a body. He leaps from the bed enraged, snatches up his robe and storms out of the room.

INT. SIR WILLIAM'S BEDROOM - DAWN

Sir William jerks mercilessly on a bell pull, then paces impatiently for it to be answered. Finally A KNOCK is heard and the door opens to admit an ELDERLY MALE SERVANT.

SIR WILLIAM
(angrily)
What are you doing here? Where's Padraig?

ELDERLY MALE SERVANT
I don't know, m'lord. With his family perhaps. I'm to wait on you tonight.

SIR WILLIAM
Find Mary Carryl and send her to me at once.

The servant bows and retreats, as Sir William rushes to his armoire and begins to throw riding clothes on his bed.

LATER

Sir William is now completely dressed in riding habit. He repeatedly smacks a riding crop against his knee-high boot. He starts impatiently back toward the bell pull just as A KNOCK sounds and Mary Carryl enters fully dressed.

SIR WILLIAM

What took you so long, Mary?

MARY CARRYL

I came as soon as I could, sir. I was not yet awake when I got your message.

SIR WILLIAM

Didn't you think the summons unusual enough to warrant haste, you stupid girl? Never mind, I've no time for excuses. Miss Sarah is not in her room. Where is she?

MARY CARRYL

(acts surprised)

Have you searched the house, sir? Perhaps Lady Betty's bedroom, to assuage her grief; or the library, to comfort herself with reading.

SIR WILLIAM

Don't play games with me, Mary! I've been to her room. One does not use pillows to camouflage one's absence to go pray or read. Speak now or you'll be out the door within the hour!

MARY CARRYL

I don't know where she is, sir. She did order a carriage last night, but it was not my place to ask questions, and she told me not to wait up. I assumed she had returned.

SIR WILLIAM

Since she hasn't returned perhaps you can *guess* where she's gone. Or have you no opinion to offer on her possible destination?

MARY CARRYL

(delaying as long as possible)

To Lady Eleanor's? I can't think where else Miss Sarah would have gone.

SIR WILLIAM

Lady Eleanor! Of course! She's behind this. Have my horse saddled at once, Mary. I'll ride to Kilkenny and get to the bottom of this.

MARY CARRYL

I'll get your breakfast started, sir.

SIR WILLIAM

Breakfast be damned! Call my groom to prepare the horses.

EXT. WATERFORD QUAY - DAWN

The coach bearing The Ladies arrives at the quay, which is almost deserted at this early hour. The DRIVER alights, helps the tired women out, and carries their bags to a small enclosed waiting area with empty benches as Frisk follows.

DRIVER

God bless, m'ladies.

SARAH

Thank you. A safe return.

INT. ENCLOSED WAITING AREA - DAWN

ELEANOR

Take advantage of the space and try to sleep, Sarah.

Sarah is shivering. Eleanor takes off her cloak and gives it to her to use as a blanket. She then sits so that Sarah can use her knee as a pillow. Frisk jumps up to lie beside Sarah. As the hours pass both Ladies doze off.

LATER

Eleanor wakes with a start to discover that a thick fog blankets the pier.

ELEANOR

Fog! Damned luck. The crossing may be delayed. But no matter. They'll never find us.

EXT. FRONT OF KILKENNY CASTLE - DAY

Sir William, his face bloated and angry, and a GROOM ride rapidly up and bring their sweating horses to a stop. They quickly dismount, and Sir William runs toward the entrance.

INT. DRAWING ROOM/KILKENNY CASTLE - DAY

Sir William, Lord Walter and Lady Butler are in heated argument. Lord Walter looks at Sir William with undisguised curiosity.

LADY BUTLER
You must stop insisting, Sir William! Eleanor isn't here I tell you.

SIR WILLIAM
I know they're together! Where could they have gone?

LADY BUTLER
(in total frustration)
What do *you* think of all this, Walter?

LORD WALTER
I think Sir William may be right.

LADY BUTLER
What on earth do you mean?

LORD WALTER
Eleanor didn't plan to return after she had assisted Sarah with Lady Betty.

LADY BUTLER
Not return? Where did she intend to go?

LORD WALTER
To England.

SIR WILLIAM
I knew it! She persuaded that silly girl to go with her. They must have gone to Waterford, it's the nearest port. Plenty of time to put a stop to that nonsense. The packets are unreliable. I'm off.

Sir William rushes out of the house.

LADY BUTLER
England? Who does Eleanor know in England?

LORD WALTER

Nobody. She decided to leave Kilkenny.

LADY BUTLER

(*furious*)

You knew this, and did nothing to stop her!

LORD WALTER

I counseled against it. She would not be dissuaded.

LADY BUTLER

How dare she do this!

LORD WALTER

You wanted her gone. She's gone.

LADY BUTLER

And was I to learn from others that my own daughter
had run away? Didn't you give one moment of
thought to my shame?

LORD WALTER

No, my dear, I didn't. Just this once I gave Eleanor
first consideration. I don't regret it. She didn't expect
Sarah to go with her. I suspect Sir William had
something to do with that decision. Now, if you'll
excuse me, I have work to do.

*Lord Walter straightens his waistcoat, smiles diffidently at
Lady Butler, and exits without a backward glance, leaving her
speechless.*

EXT. WATERFORD QUAY - DAY

*There is now much activity around the boat. Goods are being
loaded and PASSENGERS are milling around. Eleanor speaks
anxiously with the CAPTAIN.*

ELEANOR

Won't waiting on the tide mean even more delay?

CAPTAIN

What do you expect me to do, sir? I'm not God.
We'll sail as soon as we can.

ELEANOR

My companion isn't well. I implore you to let us
board at the earliest possible moment.

CAPTAIN

I shall, sir, I shall, but you must be patient.

Eleanor walks back to the now crowded enclosure where Sarah waits, looking more rested but tense.

ELEANOR

They're loading now, it won't be long.

EXT. DIRT ROAD - DAY

A coach bearing Sir William is racing frantically down the road. He sticks his head out the window to yell at the DRIVER.

SIR WILLIAM

Faster man! Faster!

EXT. WATERFORD QUAY - DAY

The coach bearing Sir William approaches rapidly and stops at the end of the quay. The passengers, now gathered in a tight group near the gangway, are slowly boarding. Eleanor, who has been anxiously looking toward the road, sees Sir William as he and the driver begin to walk toward them.

ELEANOR

How can this be? Sir William here?

Sarah is alarmed, and starts to follow Eleanor's gaze.

ELEANOR

Don't look around. He won't recognize us. We'll be on board momentarily.

As The Ladies move closer to the gangway Sir William arrives, and begins to scrutinize the passengers. He doesn't recognize The Ladies in their men's clothing, and is about to turn back when he notices Frisk, standing near Eleanor. He comes immediately up to her.

SIR WILLIAM

May I ask, sir, if you know the whereabouts of this dog's owner?

Eleanor raises her eyes only and shakes her head to indicate she does not. Sir William pauses, sensing something amiss, but not

*sure what. He stoops to pick up the dog but it twists away
from him and leaps against Sarah's leg, almost causing her to
fall. Sir William recognizes her and grasps her roughly by an
arm. Eleanor quickly reaches for Sarah as the Captain, standing
nearby, steps toward Sir William.*

CAPTAIN
Here, sir! You can't badger my passengers.

*Sir William snatches the hat from Sarah's head and her long
hair tumbles out just as Eleanor loses her grip, and Sarah falls
to the quay. The Captain and passengers look dumbfounded,
Eleanor furious, Sir William triumphant. He bends to lift Sarah
to her feet but is pushed roughly aside by Eleanor.*

ELEANOR
(menacingly)
Keep your evil hands off her! We'll not be detained!

SIR WILLIAM
You may leave for all I care. Go, and good riddance!

SARAH
(threatening convincingly)
Do as you're told, Sir William, or I'll make known
to all within earshot the treatment I've received from
you. You'll not dare show your face in public again.

*Sir William, indecisive, takes a step backward, as Eleanor and
Sarah quickly turn and board. He defiantly snatches up Frisk,
who is attempting to follow them. Sarah looks back at the wildly
wailing dog, who is now biting Sir William in an attempt to
free himself, but tearfully turns her back and continues up the
gangway.*

EXT. BOAT DECK - EVENING

*The exhausted Ladies, now in their own clothes, stand with
an arm around each other's waist as they watch the boat cast
off. The Captain passes, sees them, pauses uncertain, then,
as recognition dawns, touches his cap deferentially and stops to
talk.*

CAPTAIN

Looks as if it could be a bit stormy, Ladies. Best you stay in your cabin.

He tips his cap again and continues on his way. There is whispering and staring from other passengers on deck, but The Ladies smile amicably at them, then turn their eyes symbolically seaward, toward their destination.

INT. BOAT CABIN - NIGHT

Eleanor and Sarah, fully clothed and spooned together in a single berth, are tossed relentlessly by the pitching boat. Sarah is frightened, and slightly seasick.

SARAH

This seems more than a bit stormy.

ELEANOR

It's a rough crossing, but as near as I can judge we're within an hour of arrival.

LATER

Baggage is tossed around the cabin, and Sarah, her face ghastly white, looks terrified. Eleanor does her best to hold her steady in the turbulence. Suddenly it calms, which alarms Sarah even more.

SARAH

Are we sinking?

ELEANOR

(reassuringly)
We've passed the headland. It will be quiet now until we dock.

Sarah lies back on the berth, relief flooding her face.

EXT. DOCK - DAY

The Ladies walk unsteadily down the gangway toward a booth bearing the sign COACH.

EXT. COACH - DAY

The Ladies wait to board a coach with THREE ADULT MALES. The DRIVER is joined briefly by the Captain, and as they converse the driver's face registers surprise. Sarah notes the exchange but Eleanor doesn't. The driver returns and assists the passengers to board.

EXT. DUSTY ROAD - DAY

The Ladies and three male passengers jolt along in the moving coach. It slows and turns off the road toward a charming small country inn.

EXT. COACH - DAY

The driver opens the coach door to assist the passengers out.

DRIVER
 This is as far as we'll go tonight. A very pleasant inn.

The Ladies disembark, take the travel cases the driver hands them, and head for the inn.

INT. BEDROOM/INN - NIGHT

A cheerful fire warms the cozy, well appointed room, which has a large four poster double bed. A FEMALE SERVANT pours hot water into a large bathtub behind a screen in a corner of the room, then turns and leaves.

ELEANOR
 You first, Sarah.

LATER

Sarah sits in front of the crackling fire in her nightgown as Eleanor, also in a nightgown, comes from behind the bath screen. She walks slowly to stand behind Sarah, then reaches tentatively to place her hands on Sarah's shoulders. Without looking up Sarah reaches to grasp and draw Eleanor's hands to her breasts. Eleanor cautiously and slowly kneels beside her. Sarah turns her head and looks shyly yet with deep love into Eleanor's eyes. They kiss tenderly, then more deeply. Eleanor unsteadily stands, offers her hands to Sarah, who grasps them and also stands.

SARAH

I find myself suddenly shy.

ELEANOR

I, too... and somewhat nervous.

SARAH

Then our moods are matched.

Eleanor begins to walk slowly backward, leading Sarah to the welcoming turned-down bed. As they reach it they move to hold each other so their bodies fully touch, their arms for the first time encircling each other. They kiss more deeply. The color rises in their faces and they begin to tremble visibly. Sarah steps unsteadily backward to sit on the edge of the bed. She slowly slips off her nightgown as Eleanor stares, transfixed, at her beauty. Sarah reaches to help Eleanor remove her own gown. She looks with wonder at Eleanor, reaches to gently touch her breast, then instinctively draws her close, and buries her head in Eleanor's breasts. They tumble clumsily into bed, then move to lie side by side, joyously exploring and caressing each other.

Eleanor

Dear God, how beautiful you are.

Sarah

As are you. Unimaginably.

Eleanor leans to kiss Sarah, and she responds immediately and draws Eleanor to lie above her. They move slowly and erotically against each other, their hands and lips continue to explore as their arousal rises toward its peak. Sarah responds with complete abandon, and Eleanor watches her, enraptured, then herself reaches culmination. They collapse in exhaustion, then slowly relax, their damp bodies and faces aglow, to hold each other tightly in languid recovery.

SARAH

(*quietly, breathlessly*)

Oh Eleanor, the relief. The joy! Thank you. Thank you... Thank you, God, for this perfect love.

They continue to touch lightly and kiss tenderly, then relax in sleep, as the fire crackles brightly on.

INT. COACH - DAY

Sarah and Eleanor sit opposite each other softly smiling, basking in the glow of their love, as the coach jolts along. Two of the original male passengers have been replaced by a VULGAR WOMAN and her squirming, screaming CHILD, and one different ADULT MALE.

LATER

Hours have passed and it is near dusk. The Ladies now look exhausted, and Eleanor in particular seems irritated by the vulgar woman's failure to discipline her child.

LATER

Night has fallen, and it begins to rain, increasing to torrents, complete with thunder and lightning. The coach is wildly pitching, and barely moving. The child cries hysterically, and the vulgar woman reprimands rather than comforts it.

89

EXT. COACH - NIGHT

The coach jolts suddenly to a stop, and the rain-soaked driver flings open the passenger door.

DRIVER
All out at once! The wheels are sinking!

The passengers stumble out into the pouring rain.

DRIVER
You must all help push the coach, else it will continue to sink. Can anyone manage the horses?

ELEANOR
I can.

DRIVER
Go then.

Eleanor goes immediately to take the reins and pulls the horses forward. Sarah and the two adult male passengers join the driver at the rear of the coach and begin to push, sinking above their ankles in the mud. Slowly the wheels roll free. The vulgar woman, who has made no attempt to assist, immediately attempts to reboard. The driver stops her.

DRIVER

No one may reenter, madam. We can't resume until the road dries or we'll sink again. There was a lean-to a short distance back on the right. You'll find shelter there. I'll sit guardian here till morning.

ELEANOR

Where are you, Sarah?

SARAH

Here, Eleanor.

ELEANOR

What a foul journey. Well, let's make the best of it.

They turn with the other passengers and start down the road to the lean-to.

EXT. OVERVIEW OF VALLEY - DAY

The sun shines brightly as the coach pulls to a clearing at the side of the road and stops. The driver disembarks and opens the passenger door.

DRIVER

Horseshoe Pass, ladies and gentlemen. A good spot to stretch your legs. A lovely view of the Dee Valley.

The exhausted and filthy passengers straggle out to overlook an amazingly green valley with a small town nestled below.

SARAH

How beautiful!

ELEANOR

The first positive sign in this gloomy journey.

SARAH

(teasing)
The second. Have you forgotten so soon?

ELEANOR

(smiles, remembering)
Do you see to the left? There seems to be some sort of ruin.

SARAH

Quite a large one in fact... Driver, do you know what ruins those are?

DRIVER

Valle Crucis Abbey. Founded by the Cistercian
monks about 1201, it's believed. In ruins these many
centuries.

SARAH

Let's stop here for a few days, Eleanor. We're both
exhausted, and we promised ourselves a break.

ELEANOR

I couldn't agree more. Perhaps we'll even feel like
exploring the countryside.

DRIVER

Let's push on, ladies and gentlemen. We're almost at
Llangollen, our last stop in Wales.

INT. THE HAND INN - DAY

*The Ladies enter and are greeted by the proprietor, MR.
EDWARDS. Eleanor is tired and short tempered.*

EDWARDS

Good day, ladies. May I be of assistance.

ELEANOR

We require lodging for two nights at the minimum.

EDWARDS

Then you've come to the right place. My name is
Edwards. I'm the proprietor, and happy to report
that I have two excellent rooms available.

ELEANOR

We'll need only one room, Mr. Edwards.

EDWARDS

To be sure madam you could make do. But as luck
should have it you've struck us at low occupancy, and
we can offer the comfort of two rooms for just a
few shillings more. Much more comfortable I'm sure
you'll agree.

ELEANOR

I don't agree. My friend and I are together always,
day and night. We do not separate. We'll take your
best room only.

Edwards takes visible offense to the curtness of Eleanor's refusal, and she further offends him by taking no notice of him. He turns the register toward her to sign.

EDWARDS

As you wish, madam.

ELEANOR

(signing for both of them)

We noticed the abbey ruins as we entered the valley. Can you suggest the best path to walk and see them?

EDWARDS

Oh, it's much too far to walk, m'lady. However, I'd be happy to arrange a coach.

ELEANOR

Too far to walk? How is that possible? We passed directly beside them just minutes ago.

EDWARDS

But m'lady it would take at least the half of an hour to walk. Our local ladies don't attempt it. The dust. Most unsuitable.

ELEANOR

Then it seems we aren't so delicate as your local ladies, Mr. Edwards. Dust holds no terror for us. We shall walk. Perhaps you'd be kind enough to suggest the most pleasant path.

Edward's irritation rises with the continued rebukes. MRS. EDWARDS enters from an office directly behind him as he turns the register to read their names.

EDWARDS

Then you may also wish to visit the ruins of Castle Dinas Bran. It's little more than half an hour's stroll also. Straight uphill, but it seems that will in no way inconvenience you. I'll have Mrs. Edwards prepare directions to both. Would you oblige my dear? If you'll follow me, Lady Eleanor, Miss Ponsonby.

Edwards takes their bags and leads the way upstairs.

INT. INN OFFICE - DAY

Edwards talks animatedly to his wife.

EDWARDS
> A strange pair those two. "We do not separate." And walking about in the mud and dust. I think they aren't the ladies they pretend. Has the coach left?

MRS. EDWARDS
> I think not. Why?

EDWARDS
> I'll have a word with the driver.

INT. INN BEDROOM - DAY

Sarah parts the curtains to look out and sees Edwards talking to the coach driver. As he turns back to the inn she lets the curtains drop.

SARAH
> I think we should be more discreet in revealing our attachment, Eleanor. It may not serve our best interests to draw attention to ourselves.

ELEANOR
> *(grimacing)*
> You mean Edwards, of course. I should have been more tactful. I'm sorry, Sarah.

SARAH
> Apologies aren't necessary, but discretion is. Let's get cleaned up, that bed looks delicious.

Eleanor laughs and begins to unpack.

INT. INN OFFICE - DAY

Edwards, looking animated, bustles in.

EDWARDS
> I was right to smell a rat. Wait 'til you hear the story on those two.

He engages in rapt conversation with his eagerly listening wife.

EXT. CASTLE DINAS BRAN RUINS - DAY

The Ladies climb breathlessly hand in hand up a steep, treacherous path, and finally reach the summit.

SARAH
Edwards didn't exaggerate. It was a climb... An interesting place.

They stroll through the ruins to a point overlooking the entire town and valley. Sarah stands behind Eleanor with her arms around her. The view is stunningly beautiful and they are moved by it.

SARAH
It's wonderful to walk again.

ELEANOR
Pity the poor local ladies who must refrain from such an unpleasant pursuit.

SARAH
(laughing)
I do indeed pity them. Let's go on, I'm anxious to see the Abbey.

They turn and carefully retrace their steps down the hill.

EXT. ABBEY RUINS - DAY

The Ladies walk hand in hand past fragments of huge pillars, pausing to gently run their hands over them.

SARAH
This place seems to have a special aura.

ELEANOR
Yes, I feel it too... I think we'd best start back. The stream across the way flows toward town. Let's follow it.

They cross a dirt road and begin to follow the river.

EXT. COTTAGE - DAY

A rental agent, EVAN PUGH, posts a TO LET notice on the front of a small, white two-story cottage near the stream. The grounds are well tended, with many trees and flowers, including

94

some beautiful roses. The hill on which Dinas Bran sits is visible high in the background.

ELEANOR

Good afternoon.

PUGH

(startled)

Good afternoon to you! I don't often meet ladies strolling in this area.

ELEANOR

So we've been told. Such beautiful roses. A charming cottage.

PUGH

It is, indeed. Not easy to let, however, as it's perceived to be outside the town. Sad. It's so pleasant. And inexpensive – –

SARAH

How inexpensive?

Both Eleanor and Pugh are surprised by Sarah's question.

PUGH

It depends on the length of the lease, m'lady.

SARAH

I'd be interested to know. If it's not inconvenient?

PUGH

Not in the least. My pleasure. Let me introduce myself. My name is Evan Pugh.

SARAH

I'm Sarah Ponsonby. My friend, Lady Eleanor Butler.

Pugh touches his hat respectfully, takes some papers out of his pocket and shows them to Sarah, as Eleanor wanders off to look at the roses.

SARAH

Let's look inside, Eleanor.

INT. COTTAGE - DAY

The rooms are small, but clean and charming. The essential furniture, of good quality, is already in place. They look around the living room and kitchen downstairs.

SARAH

> May we go upstairs?

PUGH

> By all means. Take your time.

He doesn't accompany them upstairs, where there are two bedrooms. The larger contains a rather plain four poster double bed. Both are obviously entranced with the cottage.

ELEANOR

> This is exactly what we'll look for in England.

EXT. COTTAGE - DAY

Pugh tips his hat good-bye, and Sarah and Eleanor resume their walk toward town.

INT. DESK/THE HAND - DAY

Eleanor is settling her account with a very correct Edwards.

EDWARDS

> You've enjoyed your stay, m'lady?

ELEANOR

> Yes indeed, Mr. Edwards. Especially our walks...
> What time does the coach leave tomorrow?

EDWARDS

> Not 'til noon.

ELEANOR

> Oh, dear. That is awkward, checkout being so early.
> May we may keep our room until we leave?

EDWARDS

> Half board for the half day.

ELEANOR

> *(annoyed)*
> I didn't realize a delayed departure would so
> inconvenience you, Mr. Edwards. We'll oblige and
> wait in the lounge. Good night to you.

EDWARDS

> As you wish. Good night, Lady Eleanor.

INT. INN BEDROOM - DAY

Eleanor enters.

ELEANOR

What an odious man that Edwards is!

She's alarmed to notice that Sarah looks quite upset.

ELEANOR

Sarah, what's wrong? You haven't been yourself all day.

SARAH

We must settle here in Llangollen, Eleanor. I know my saying this will displease you, but it must be said.

ELEANOR

England is better suited to our needs, Sarah. When you see it you'll understand.

SARAH

We can't afford city living.

ELEANOR

Of course we can! My annuity will be ample if we're careful. And father will help.

SARAH

But what if your father dies, do you trust your mother to assist us? Your family has no legal obligation to you. Anything you receive will be provided at their pleasure, and we've displeased them greatly. We can count on nothing.

ELEANOR

Your points are well taken, Sarah, but there's no urgency for a decision.

SARAH

I disagree. You've entrusted me with our reserves, and I must tell you they're dwindling rapidly. We must settle soon and become self sufficient if we hope to survive. That cottage is perfect.

Eleanor looks deeply at Sarah, who remains determined. She sighs and gives in.

ELEANOR

I know that look.
(uncertainly)
The cottage has all we need to get started, and the kitchen is complete.

SARAH

You loved the gardens, and there's plenty of room for crops.

ELEANOR

All right, we'll settle here. At least for now.

SARAH

(deeply relieved)
Thank you, Eleanor. I know we've made the right decision.

ELEANOR

I'll have to revisit Mr. Edwards and tell him he'll have the pleasure of our company for a few more days.

As Eleanor exits the room Sarah sits down, her face registering exhaustion and relief.

INT. REALTY OFFICE - DAY

Sarah watches as Eleanor signs two copies of the lease. Pugh hands one copy back to Eleanor with the cottage keys.

PUGH

"Pob lwc yn eich plas newydd," Ladies.

SARAH

What does that mean, Mr. Pugh?

PUGH

A Welsh blessing. "Every luck in your new home."

SARAH

"Plas Newydd." It has a lovely ring doesn't it, Eleanor? That's what we'll call our cottage. Plas Newydd.

INT. COTTAGE BEDROOM - DAY

Eleanor is awake, propped on an elbow looking lovingly at a still sleeping Sarah, who stretches and wakens to her smile. Eleanor

98

leans over to kiss her, and Sarah reaches to invite intimacy.
Eleanor gently pushes her away.

ELEANOR
We've had our first wonderful night in our new
home. Now it's down to business. We must go to
town to set up accounts and get supplies.

SARAH
Yes, that's a priority. But we'll have tonight – –

ELEANOR
And the next, and the next.

Eleanor throws back the covers and gets up quickly, playfully
pulling Sarah after her.

EXT. STREET - DAY

The Ladies walk past SEVERAL WOMEN to whom they say
good day, but who do not acknowledge them. SEVERAL MEN
they pass respond with the tip of a hat but also do not stop
to speak.

ELEANOR
Not overly friendly in this town, are they?

INT. PARRY'S GROCERY SHOP - DAY

The proprietor, MRS. PARRY, is conversing with SEVERAL
FEMALE CUSTOMERS, who step aside as The Ladies enter.

MRS. PARRY
Good day, ladies.

ELEANOR
Good day. Mrs. Parry, I presume. I'm Eleanor
Butler, and this is my friend, Miss Ponsonby.

MRS. PARRY
I'm acquainted with your names, Lady Eleanor. It's a
small town, after all. You'll be wanting to know about
an account, no doubt.

ELEANOR
Our exact mission, Mrs. Parry.

MRS. PARRY

I operate on a cash basis only.

ELEANOR

Cash only?

MRS. PARRY

I treat all equally.

Sarah is looking directly at an open account book which lies facing Mrs. Parry on the counter. Following Sarah's gaze, she reaches over and nonchalantly closes it.

SARAH

Cash will be acceptable, Mrs. Parry. Providing our good custom will be honored by a reconsideration of terms as we establish ourselves.

MRS. PARRY

I'll do my best. But credit would be an exception. Will you be needing anything today, ladies?

ELEANOR

(opening her purse)

Potatoes, flour, salt, yeast, tea. Cheese if you have some.

MRS. PARRY

I'll have my boy deliver it before noon. He'll bring the bill with him then.

ELEANOR

Thank you. We'd appreciate that... Well, good day Mrs. Parry.

As The Ladies turn to leave Eleanor notices Mrs. Edwards among the customers.

ELEANOR

Hello, Mrs. Edwards.

MRS. EDWARDS

Good day, Lady Eleanor. Miss Ponsonby.

Eleanor hesitates, sensing coldness in the greeting. As she and Sarah leave the store CONVERSATION begins inside.

EXT. STREET - DAY

ELEANOR
(grimly)
We're off to a poor start, Sarah.

SARAH
(looking remorseful)
They've heard of our elopement, Eleanor. I was aware, but hoped it would cause no problem. It was wrong of me not to tell you.

Eleanor stops and looks at Sarah in astonishment. She thinks silently for a few moments. Then sighs.

ELEANOR
So we aren't to be graced with even a day of anonymity. Never mind, all strangers must prove themselves, why should we be an exception? God knows we're unusual enough. Let's get home. Your lessons today will be on planting potatoes, and making bread.

SARAH
(enormously relieved by Eleanor's attitude)
My lessons are taking a more practical turn. Sir William would be delighted to know I've truly sunk to being "in trade."

Eleanor laughs, and they link arms and continue homeward.

EXT. COTTAGE VEGETABLE GARDEN - DAY

The sweating and red-faced Ladies, dressed like peasants, kneel side by side near a freshly hoed area. Two soil-stained hoes lie to one side. A bag of potatoes is lying beside them, as Eleanor demonstrates how to plant them.

ELEANOR
Cut each piece so that it has an eye, and plant it two to three inches deep, about 10 inches apart.

SARAH
That's it?

ELEANOR

> The rest is up to God... and the weather. Potatoes are sturdy. They won't disappoint us. We'll do cabbage, turnips and carrots next. I'll order seeds tomorrow.

INT. MR. JONES' SEED/FEED/FERTILIZER STORE - DAY

Eleanor speaks in frustration to the proprietor, MR. JONES.

ELEANOR

> It's been over a week since I ordered, Mr. Jones. We need the seed now if we're to have produce for the winter. What's the delay?

MR. JONES

> *(blatantly lying)*
> It's most unusual, Lady Eleanor. I put the order in immediately.

ELEANOR

> Cancel the order. I'll go to Wrexham for them myself.

Eleanor smiles knowingly, turns without haste, and exits.

EXT. COTTAGE VEGETABLE GARDEN - DAY

Green potato shoots are already several inches high, and an additional area has been hoed and furrowed. The exhausted Ladies are planting seed when a cart unexpectedly lumbers into the drive. As it stops they are astonished to see Mary Carryl disembark with Frisk, who runs to Sarah to be picked up.

SARAH

> Mary Carryl! I can't believe my eyes! What are you doing here?

MARY CARRYL

> I had a little put by, Miss Sarah. I've come to stay if you and Lady Eleanor will have me.

SARAH

> Let you stay? Oh, Mary! I'm afraid you've put yourself in a bad position. This is no grand mansion you've come to.

MARY CARRYL

> I wasn't born in one, Miss Sarah.

ELEANOR

The work here is endless, Mary. We've become lady farmers in order to survive.

MARY CARRYL

I've some experience in farming, m'lady. Where do you want me to start?

SARAH

Let me get you settled first, Mary.

ELEANOR

I'll get back to work. Welcome Mary. God bless you.

Eleanor turns tearfully away as Sarah and Mary enter the cottage.

EXT. COTTAGE VEGETABLE GARDEN - DAY

A large area now has fully grown cabbage, turnips, carrots, and potatoes ready for harvesting. An exhausted Sarah, Eleanor and Mary Carryl work steadily. Sarah suddenly sits in the middle of the field.

ELEANOR
(anxiously)
What's the matter, Sarah?

SARAH

We haven't even started a cellar yet! We're running out of time, not to mention strength. We've got to have some help.

ELEANOR

You know how hard I've tried.

SARAH

I'm going to see the vicar. He's the only person whose conscience may not let him refuse us.

ELEANOR

Don't count on it. But I agree it's worth a try.

INT. ST. COLLEN'S CHURCH - DAY

Sarah talks with the vicar, MR. PROTHEROW.

MR. PROTHEROW

I do know of one young fellow. A bit too fond of the drink, I'm afraid. He may be difficult.

SARAH

> We can deal with that, Mr. Protherow. I do thank
> you. We're desperately in need of help.

MR. PROTHEROW

> His name is Rown. I'll get word to him today. I've
> been hoping to see you and Lady Eleanor at services,
> Miss Ponsonby.

SARAH

> We work without stop, vicar. We'll be here as soon as
> we can spare the time.

EXT. COTTAGE - DAY

*Eleanor, Sarah and the gardener, ROWN, examine a now
completed cellar.*

SARAH

> Well, Rown, we won't starve this year.

ROWN

> No, Miss.

ELEANOR

> It's time to find a cow, some lambs, maybe a hog or
> two. How's the budget holding up, Sarah?

SARAH

> How much will all this cost?

ELEANOR

> I've no idea, but we'll know before nightfall. Let's go
> to Wrexham. It's time you learned how to bargain.
> Perhaps you'll enjoy it more than I do.

SARAH

> And be better at it.

ELEANOR

> *(laughs)*
> That's a possibility I hadn't thought of.

EXT. COTTAGE VEGETABLE GARDEN - DAY

*There is evidence that several seasons have passed as landscaping
has been started and fruit trees are in bloom. Eleanor is
supervising Rown and an additional LABORER as they work in
the garden. Eleanor notices a man approaching on foot, shades*

her eyes to look, then runs to greet the visitor. As the two
approach the cottage Sarah exits and recognizes Geoffrey, who
grins and embraces her.

ELEANOR
We'd have been better prepared if we'd known the
date you were passing through to London, Geoffrey.

GEOFFREY
You'd have put yourself out, and that isn't necessary.

Geoffrey looks around, obviously impressed.

GEOFFREY
You haven't done it justice in your letters. It's
beautiful.

ELEANOR
Sarah, have Mary get tea ready. I'll give Geoffrey a
quick tour. I assume a budding politician still has
interest in farming?

GEOFFREY
You've got it backwards, Eleanor. Ask the farmer why
he takes time for politics. Speeches put no meat on
the table.

Eleanor and Geoffrey turn toward the back of the cottage as
Sarah reenters.

EXT. ANIMAL STALL - DAY

Geoffrey and Eleanor are leaning on a stall which contains a
cow and several lambs. Two hogs are in a nearby sty, and several
chickens are walking around.

ELEANOR
We have enough to meet our obligations.

GEOFFREY
You've only to ask, Eleanor.

ELEANOR
We must manage on our own or we'll have proved
nothing.

GEOFFREY
Is it so necessary to prove?

ELEANOR

Yes. To ourselves, our families, the townspeople. But I thank you for the offer, I won't forget it.

INT. COTTAGE DRAWING ROOM - DAY

Sarah, Eleanor and Geoffrey are seated.

SARAH

Tell us the latest about Beatrice and the little one.

GEOFFREY

She's won mother over completely with her charm. Our Kevin is a sturdy lad... And we're expecting again.

ELEANOR

Congratulations, Geoffrey! I knew you'd be a match. It's good to hear of happy pairings besides our own.

SARAH

Have Eleanor show you our library, Geoffrey. We're quite proud of it.

Geoffrey and Eleanor walk to a wall of well-stocked bookshelves. Mary Carryl enters, sets down a tea tray, and Sarah begins to pour.

ELEANOR

Father was kind enough to send all my things. We add books as we can.

GEOFFREY

I find many titles I envy you for.

ELEANOR

They bring the world to us, Geoffrey, since we aren't able, nor do we any longer care, to go to it.

They return and sit for tea.

GEOFFREY

Any gentry nearby?

SARAH

Some. Our paths haven't crossed.

GEOFFREY

I'd have thought they might seek you out.

ELEANOR

To the world we're anonymous. It suits us.

SARAH

Have you news of Nigel?

GEOFFREY

Good news. He's been made vicar. He remains solitary, attending to his work. But he seems content.

SARAH

I wrote several times but received no answer.

GEOFFREY

Deep wounds take time to heal, Sarah.

SARAH

Remember us to him when you see him.

GEOFFREY

Of course I will.

EXT. COUNTRY ESTATE - DAY

BRYNKINALT, the estate of 65 year old LADY DUNGANNON. A carriage brings a middle aged man, EWAN WILLIAMS, and nine year old ARTHUR WELLESLEY to the front entrance.

INT. DRAWING ROOM - DAY

A FOOTMAN enters the very elegantly furnished room and announces the arrival.

FOOTMAN

Mr. Williams and Master Wellesley, m'lady.

Ewan and Arthur enter the drawing room.

EWAN

Here he is, Lady Dungannon.

LADY DUNGANNON

Come in, come in. Thank you, Ewan. My goodness, Arthur, how you've grown. Come here and give your grandmother a big hug.

Arthur walks to Lady Dungannon and hugs her.

LADY DUNGANNON

How does it feel to be back, Arthur?

ARTHUR

I'm very happy to be back, grandmama. I've been looking forward to the ponies.

LADY DUNGANNON

Ponies! Well I can see you haven't changed as much as I thought. We have a new boy to help in the stable. His name is Timmy. He'll ride with you whenever you wish.

ARTHUR

May I go today, grandmama? I'd very much like to go now while it's still light.

LADY DUNGANNON

Yes, you may go now. But change your clothes before you leave. And be back in good time for dinner.

ARTHUR

I will. I promise. Thank you, grandmama.

Lady Dungannon shakes her head affectionately as Arthur excitedly runs out of the room.

LADY DUNGANNON

Sit a few minutes and tell me the news, Ewan.

EWAN

Well, let me see. The roads have been repaired and the ride over is much improved. The new vicar has arrived, and seems pleasant enough. But of course the biggest news concerns our new neighbors.

LADY DUNGANNON

New neighbors? I haven't heard of any new neighbors.

EWAN

Nor had I. They live very quietly outside Llangollen town I'm told.

LADY DUNGANNON

So now you shall have the pleasure of telling all. Who are they?

EWAN

Two ladies from Ireland.

LADY DUNGANNON

Two ladies? From Ireland you say?

EWAN

A Lady Eleanor Butler, and a Miss Ponsonby. A strange pair it seems.

LADY DUNGANNON

Strange? How?

EWAN

It's widely reported they eloped together. And there's speculation concerning large sums reported missing by their respective families. But here, let me read you excerpts from the *Post*. For you see, I don't make this up.

Ewan takes a copy of the GENERAL EVENING POST newspaper out of his pocket, opens it, and begins to read.

EWAN

"EXTRAORDINARY FEMALE AFFECTION. Lady Eleanor Butler and Miss Ponsonby, the daughters of the two great Irish families whose names they bear, have recently retired from society into a certain Welch Vale. Lady Eleanor had several offers of marriage, all of which she rejected. Miss Ponsonby, her particular friend and companion, was suspected to be the bar to matrimonial union, and it was thought proper to separate them." But here, see for yourself.

Ewan hands the paper to a dumbfounded Lady Dungannon, who reads silently for a few moments, then aloud.

LADY DUNGANNON

"Lady Eleanor was confined. However, the two Ladies found means to elope together... Lady Eleanor is tall and masculine. She wears always a riding habit, and appears in all respects as a young man. She superintends the gardens and the rest of the grounds. Miss Ponsonby, on the contrary, is effeminate and beautiful, and does the duties and honours of the house." Is this true, Ewan? What are they like?

EWAN

As I said, I've never met them. But the article is quite specific.

LADY DUNGANNON

But who has written this? Such outrageous charges! Scarcely believable. Still, very titillating. I shall make it a point to meet them. They are titled, after all.

EXT. STABLE - DAY

The stable boy, TIMMY, is raking hay as Arthur enters.

ARTHUR

Are you Timmy, then? Lady Dungannon said you would ride with me.

TIMMY

Aye, Master Arthur. I'm Timmy. I am instructed to go with you whenever you like.

ARTHUR

I wish to go now. I haven't been on a pony since my last visit.

The two boys lead out and begin to saddle two ponies. Timmy is more skilled at this, but Arthur is pushy and wants to do it alone. He is excited and anxious to start riding.

ARTHUR

Where shall we ride, Timmy?

TIMMY

I know the way to Llangollen best... We can ride there and see the strange ladies!

ARTHUR

What strange ladies?

TIMMY

Two ladies from Ireland. My mam says they're strange... I think they may be witches!

ARTHUR

Witches? What do they look like?

TIMMY

I haven't seen them. They mostly stay at their cottage outside the town. But I know the way. They can't catch us if we're on the ponies.

ARTHUR

Real witches! Excellent, Timmy. Let's go!

They mount their ponies and walk them away from the stable. Arthur impatiently starts to trot his pony. Timmy hurries to catch up, then takes the lead to show the way.

INT. KITCHEN/ PLAS NEWYDD - DAY

Mary Carryl is busy working at the fireplace as Sarah enters with the General Evening Post *in her hand. She is obviously distraught. The dog Frisk follows her in.*

SARAH

Have you seen Lady Eleanor?

MARY CARRYL

Out again with Rown over some planting not done to her satisfaction.

Mary notices Sarah's distress.

MARY CARRYL

Is everything all right, Miss Sarah?

SARAH

Some unpleasant news, nothing to concern yourself with, Mary.

Sarah turns to leave and Frisk begins to follow.

SARAH

Stay, Frisk.

EXT. RIVERBANK/REAR OF COTTAGE - DAY

A narrow rustic bridge crosses the river about 50 yards upstream from a bench on which The Ladies sit. Eleanor is holding the General Evening Post.

SARAH

Why would anyone write such lies about us? Our life is of no consequence to anyone but ourselves.

They sit, silent and deeply shocked, on the bench.

EXT. OPPOSITE RIVERBANK - DAY

Arthur and Timmy ride along the river.

ARTHUR
(impatiently)
Where *are* these witches, Timmy? We've been riding nearly an hour.

TIMMY
Just a short distance now, Master Arthur.

They come abreast of The Ladies and stop behind some trees to look across at them. Timmy is afraid, but Arthur is curious and bold.

ARTHUR
I can't see them from here, Timmy. I'm going across that bridge. They can't catch me if I'm riding.

TIMMY
Don't do that, Master Arthur! It's said they eat small boys.

ARTHUR
Rubbish, Timmy! Have any boys been missing?

TIMMY
I've not heard of any.

ARTHUR
Of course you haven't! Witches eat only snakes and lizards. You're so stupid, Timmy! I'm going over.

Arthur turns upstream and starts his horse across the bridge. It's terrified of the rushing water and rears up, tossing him, screaming, into the swiftly flowing stream, then backs off the bridge. The Ladies, startled, look up and jump quickly to their feet, as Arthur is washed downstream toward them. Eleanor quickly wades into the river to rescue him, and drags him with difficulty to the riverbank.

SARAH
Rown! Rown! Come quickly.

Rown appears running and helps pull Arthur, who doesn't appear to be breathing, out of the river.

ELEANOR

Bottom up. Quickly, Rown!

Eleanor pounds Arthur on his back. Water pours from his mouth and he begins to cough and sputter, his face regaining color. He's bleeding from a small head wound. Sarah reaches to her petticoat, rips off its bottom trim and wraps it around his head. Rown picks the boy up and walks quickly toward the cottage as The Ladies follow.

EXT. OPPOSITE RIVERBANK - DAY

Timmy watches the rescue, panic stricken, then turns his horse and races off, Arthur's horse following.

INT. KITCHEN/PLAS NEWYDD - DAY

Rown enters with Arthur and lays him on a settee. Mary, startled, reaches immediately for towels and a blanket.

ELEANOR

Do you recognize him, Rown?

ROWN

No, m'lady. I've not seen him about the town. Doesn't look like a local lad. Better dressed than most around here. Quite the young gentleman, I'd say.

SARAH

There was another boy with him who rode off after the rescue. I expect we'll know soon enough who he is. Thank you, Rown. You must change, Eleanor. Help me with the boy, Mary.

Eleanor and Rown exit as Sarah and Mary begin to undress Arthur.

EXT. LADY DUNGANNON'S COUNTRY ESTATE - DAY

Timmy rides wildly to the front entrance of Brynkinalt, with Arthur's horse following. Lady Dungannon, who has been sitting on the verandah, leaps to her feet in alarm.

LADY DUNGANNON

Timmy! What's happened? Where's Master Arthur?

TIMMY

The witches have him! Oh, Lady Dungannon, he wouldn't listen. He went across that bridge – –

LADY DUNGANNON

Slowly, Timmy, slowly. Start at the beginning.

INT. KITCHEN/PLAS NEWYDD - DAY

Sarah sits anxiously near the unconscious Arthur, while Eleanor stands behind her. He begins to groan, and slowly opens his eyes, which focus and fill with terror. He senses his head bandage and reaches to touch it, obviously in pain.

SARAH

(enormously relieved)
You cut yourself when you fell off your horse.

Arthur is too terrified to speak. He suddenly realizes he is naked and grasps the blanket, pulling it tightly to his chin.

SARAH

Your clothes are drying by the fire. You were soaked after your adventure. Can you tell us who you are? We should send word to your parents.

ARTHUR

(whispers)
Arthur Wellesley.

SARAH

Where do you live, Arthur?

ARTHUR

Ireland.

SARAH.

You didn't ride here from Ireland?

ARTHUR

From grandmama's.

SARAH

From grandmama's. You're a man of few words, Arthur Wellesley. Who is grandmama?

ARTHUR

Lady Dungannon.

SARAH

Ah! And your friend?

Arthur looks totally blank, and only slightly less terrified.

SARAH

Didn't we see another boy with you?

ARTHUR

Timmy. He works in the stable.

SARAH

Then we needn't worry. I've no doubt he went directly back for assistance. Well, I think perhaps the chocolate now, Mary.

Mary pours some hot chocolate into a mug and brings it to Arthur. He reaches out tentatively and takes the mug, then looks fearfully inside at the chocolate.

SARAH

Don't you like chocolate, Arthur? We can make tea. But you must have something warm.

ARTHUR

You drink chocolate?

Arthur includes Eleanor in his glance for the first time, and sensing this she answers.

ELEANOR

Why, yes, we do. In fact I'll have a cup with you.

SARAH

This is Lady Eleanor, Arthur. You have her to thank for pulling you out of the river.

ARTHUR

Lady Eleanor?

SARAH

Lady Eleanor Butler. And my name is Sarah Ponsonby.

Frisk jumps up and begins to lick Arthur's face. He's startled at first, then thrilled by the dog. His fear is now almost completely gone.

SARAH

> This is Frisk. He's been impatient for you to wake up so he could say hello.

Frisk settles down by Arthur, who finishes his chocolate and begins to doze off. Sarah takes the mug and covers him back up.

SARAH

> Just as well he rest a while.

INT. DRAWING ROOM/PLAS NEWYDD - LATE AFTERNOON

Eleanor and Sarah are seated. The SOUND OF A CARRIAGE is heard.

ELEANOR

> That will be for Arthur. I'll go.

EXT. COTTAGE - DAY

Eleanor exits the cottage as an elegant coach rolls to a stop. A very worried Lady Dungannon exits. Eleanor is taken aback.

ELEANOR

> Lady Dungannon? We have Master Arthur here. A cut on the head but otherwise none the worse for wear.

LADY DUNGANNON

> Thank God for that. And you are?

ELEANOR

> Eleanor Butler.

LADY DUNGANNON

> Lady Eleanor. Thank you. Where is he?

ELEANOR

> Sleeping at the moment. Please, this way.

INT. KITCHEN/PLAS NEWYDD - DAY

Lady Dungannon follows Eleanor into the kitchen and looks at the sleeping Arthur. She is emotionally drained.

SARAH

> This has been a shock. Come rest for a few minutes. Mary will bring tea.

LADY DUNGANNON

Thank you. Most kind.

INT. DRAWING ROOM/PLAS NEWYDD - DAY

LADY DUNGANNON

I learned of your arrival only today. I'm glad to meet you so soon, but would have preferred different circumstances, of course. You haven't been injured yourselves from this event?

ELEANOR

Not at all.

LADY DUNGANNON

You have my earnest thanks for your quick action. Arthur tends to be adventurous, but he's outdone himself with this escapade.
(notices the newspaper on a table)
I see you've read that libelous *Evening Post* article. Gossip sells, but memories are mercifully short, thank God. One can only go on. Rise above it.

ELEANOR

(bitterly)
Easier said than done, unfortunately.

LADY DUNGANNON

Yes. You do well to remind me that this is so. I meant no disrespect. I'm quite aware of the humiliation, having been subjected to attack myself on several occasions. I apologize if I've offended you.

ELEANOR

No apology is needed, Lady Dungannon. My bitterness was for the event, not your comment.

LADY DUNGANNON

Yet some good may come of it. You see I'm quite old fashioned. I believe that one good turn deserves another, and I'd be pleased if you'd let me arrange your introduction. I think it fair to say, thanks to the *Post*, that no invitation will be refused. May I have the privilege of doing this?

SARAH

(shocked with surprise)
The privilege would be ours, Lady Dungannon.

ELEANOR

It's a very generous offer.

LADY DUNGANNON

Don't think I act simply out of gratitude. I see you are deserving.

Mary arrives with the tea, and Eleanor begins to pour.

MARY CARRYL

Master Arthur is awake. Shall I get him dressed?

SARAH

Yes, thank you, Mary.

LATER

Mary reenters with a very unsteady Arthur. Frisk follows him as he goes to sit near Lady Dungannon.

LADY DUNGANNON

Well, Arthur, this has been quite a day. You're lucky to be alive.

ARTHUR

It was an accident, grandmama. My pony wouldn't behave.

LADY DUNGANNON

That isn't what I've surmised from Timmy's account. A narrow bridge over a rushing stream. I shouldn't care for it if I were a pony. It was reckless, Arthur.

ARTHUR

I'm sorry, grandmama. I won't do it again.

LADY DUNGANNON

Yes, you will. Or something equally as unwise. It's in your nature to take risks... It's time we went, Arthur. Thank Lady Eleanor and Miss Ponsonby for your rescue.

ARTHUR

Thank you very much Lady Eleanor, Miss Ponsonby. May I visit again to see Frisk?

SARAH

Of course you may, but try the front door next time.

LADY DUNGANNON

I'll stop on my way home to see Edwards about your introductory evening.

ELEANOR

Edwards of The Hand?

LADY DUNGANNON

You know him of course?

SARAH

Yes, we're well acquainted.

LADY DUNGANNON

Then we'll have only to set the date. I'll let you know as soon as all is arranged. Thank you again for your quick action, and your hospitality.

INT. THE HAND INN - DAY

Edwards is at the desk as Lady Dungannon enters.

LADY DUNGANNON

Good day, Edwards. I wish to book your services.

EDWARDS

Of course, Lady Dungannon.

LADY DUNGANNON

I'll be hosting an introductory evening for Lady Eleanor Butler and Miss Ponsonby, and I'll need your assistance.

EDWARDS

Lady Eleanor and Miss Ponsonby?

LADY DUNGANNON

You know them, don't you? They said you were well acquainted.

EDWARDS

Of course, m'lady. We most certainly are.

LADY DUNGANNON

They're quite wonderful, don't you think? So gracious. A wonderful addition to our little community.

EDWARDS

Indeed they are. And how may I help?

LADY DUNGANNON
This is what I had in mind.

INT. OFFICE/HAND - DAY

Edwards and Mrs. Edwards are in heated argument.

EDWARDS
How was I to know they would become favorites?

MRS. EDWARDS
They're gentry. That should have been enough. Why did I listen to you? You must make amends. And quickly.

EDWARDS
I must make amends? What about you?

MRS. EDWARDS
You'll speak for both of us. This is what you must do.

EXT. COTTAGE - DAY

Eleanor and Sarah walk near the front of the cottage as Edwards drives up in his chaise. He doffs his hat respectfully as he steps down.

ELEANOR
Mr. Edwards. This is a surprise.

EDWARDS
I've not come at an inconvenient time?

ELEANOR
Not at all.

EDWARDS
I had a matter I wished to discuss.

ELEANOR
By all means. Why don't we go inside? More comfortable, I think.

INT. DRAWING ROOM/PLAS NEWYDD - DAY

Edwards is seated bolt upright on the edge of his chair, holding his hat by its brim in front of his knees.

ELEANOR
What's on your mind, Mr. Edwards?

EDWARDS

As you no doubt know I'm assisting Lady Dungannon
with your introductory evening. In the course of
doing so it's occurred to Mrs. Edwards and myself
that you'll need transportation to the event. I've
come to offer my coach and services.

SARAH

That's very kind of you, Mr. Edwards. But do I
understand correctly? This is not a solicitation. It's
an offer of your coach and driver for the evening?

Edwards sits even more bolt upright.

EDWARDS

Only partly correct, madam. I myself will drive. I'll
not trust your safety to anyone but myself after dark.

SARAH

That's most generous of you, Mr. Edwards.

EDWARDS

You accept, then?

SARAH

Lady Eleanor?

ELEANOR

Very gracious. We accept your offer with pleasure,
Mr. Edwards.

EDWARDS

Well, that's it, then! Mrs. Edwards will be relieved
you've placed yourselves in my care.

ELEANOR

I've no doubt she will, Mr. Edwards.

EXT. COTTAGE - DAY

Eleanor and Sarah watch Edwards' coach until it disappears.

ELEANOR

Our days are suddenly full of surprises... Now, Sarah,
let's talk about our outfits for the party. We'll never
have a more opportune occasion to use the reserves
we've laid by. Let me show you what I had in mind.

INT. COTTAGE - DAY

Eleanor opens a French fashion magazine. She thumbs through it, locates the page she wants, and shows it to Sarah.

ELEANOR
Here. What do you think?

SARAH
I've never seen anything like it. It's very different.

ELEANOR
We're different, and they've never seen anything like us. We should be distinctive.

SARAH
You have a point. Why shouldn't we?

EXT. VALLE CRUCIS ABBEY - NIGHT

The light from a full moon spotlights the massive ruined pillars and walls of the Abbey. MUSICIANS are playing soft classical music as the GUESTS, representative of upper gentry and nobility in their finest, stroll about. Included are BARON AND BARONESS CHESTERTON, ADMIRAL ORMSBY, in full naval dress, and LORD AND LADY PRENTICE. Liveried SERVANTS are passing trays of wine and delicacies. Edwards' chaise appears, and stops near the entrance. He quickly disembarks to assist The Ladies out. They are wearing identical black outfits, consisting of tuxedo type hip-length fitted jackets, full length skirts with a small bustle at the back, ruffled white blouses, and medium height beaver top hats, softened with a veil on one side which drops from the top to an area near the brim. They are greeted by Lady Dungannon and Arthur, who immediately takes Sarah's hand. Lady Dungannon begins to introduce The Ladies. People are anxious to meet them, and eagerly wait to be introduced.

LADY DUNGANNON
Baron and Baroness Chesterton.

ELEANOR
It's a pleasure to meet you, Baron, Baroness. We've heard of your magnificent stables.

BARON CHESTERTON
Then we must issue a standing invitation for you to come see them. We'll send our carriage to fetch you anytime it's convenient.

LADY DUNGANNON
> Admiral Ormsby. Lady Eleanor Butler and Miss Sarah Ponsonby.

ELEANOR
> A pleasure to meet you, Admiral. We've been reading of your success in stopping that scoundrel John Paul Jones from sinking our merchant ships.

ADMIRAL ORMSBY
> Why, thank you! Devilish clever mariner. Always seems to be in three places at once, but we've had some success.

Arthur diverts Sarah's attention to whisper to her.

ARTHUR
> I'm going to be a soldier when I grow up, Sarah.

SARAH
> It's a dangerous occupation, Arthur. Be very sure it's what you want. You have plenty of time to decide.

ARTHUR
> I won't change my mind.

LADY DUNGANNON
> Lord and Lady Prentice.

LADY PRENTICE
> Delighted. Your outfits are stunning, ladies. You must tell me about them.

Sarah begins to model as Eleanor points out different details of her outfit. Sarah raises her skirt to show off her boots. As the party continues The Ladies are seen laughing and interacting with many people, sometimes together, sometimes separately.

SUPER: LLANGOLLEN - 1829

INT. TEA SHOP/LLANGOLLEN - DAY

Eleanor, a frail 77, Sarah, 71, and the Duke of Wellington, 61, in civilian clothing, are enjoying afternoon tea together. The TEAROOM STAFF attend to them as if they were royalty.

ELEANOR

What a life we've had, Arthur! We thought we'd have to bring the world to us through our books – –

SARAH

(smiling with reminiscence)
But it came to us instead.

DUKE OF WELLINGTON

It's really remarkable. The entire continent has heard of you. Waterloo is long forgotten and I'm more in demand as your friend than on my own merit these days.

ELEANOR

(teasing)
I hope that isn't why you continue to visit your two old friends.

DUKE OF WELLINGTON

I come because they're brilliant; because they know everyone and everything, and are wiser in the ways of the world than anyone else of my acquaintance... Did I remember to mention that I love them?

SARAH

What a beautiful tribute, Arthur.

Suddenly Sarah and Arthur notice that Eleanor seems to be having trouble keeping her balance. She loses consciousness and topples sideways on her chair just as the Duke reaches over to prevent her from falling. With assistance from Sarah he lays her gently on her side on the floor. Pandemonium reigns as the news of her collapse spreads through the shop, and into the street.

EXT. STREET OUTSIDE TEA SHOP - DAY

The streets are lined with deeply worried TOWNSPEOPLE as Eleanor is carried out on a litter by TWO BEARERS. Sarah, in a state of shock, walks on one side of the litter, the Duke, showing deep concern, on the other. They turn toward Plas Newydd.

INT. BEDROOM/PLAS NEWYDD - NIGHT

Eleanor is lying propped on her side in her own four poster bed from Kilkenny. Sarah sits at the bedside holding her limp hand, and smoothing her hair. Eleanor slowly opens her eyes and begins to focus, recognizing Sarah.

ELEANOR
(in a slurred whisper)
How I have loved you, Sarah. Love you still.

SARAH
Rest, my darling.

Eleanor closes her eyes, then wearily opens them again to stare at Sarah, whom she no longer seems able to see. She begins to mumble the 23rd Psalm.

ELEANOR
"Lord is my shepherd... shall not want... maketh... green pastures..."

Eleanor's eyes close again, and she loses consciousness. Sarah picks up the Psalm where Eleanor has left off.

SARAH
"Yea, though I walk through the valley of the shadow of death, I will fear no evil; for thou art with me; thy rod and thy staff they comfort me..."

The DOCTOR enters, examines Eleanor's pupils, shakes his head, and as he quietly leaves, her respirations change from shallow and rapid to deep and infrequent.

SARAH
"Surely goodness and mercy shall follow me all the days of my life; and I will dwell in the house of the Lord forever."

Eleanor dies quietly. Sarah stands, crying but controlled, and goes to look out the bedroom window. The lawn is crowded with townspeople holding burning candles or lanterns. She slowly closes the shutters.

EXT. PLAS NEWYDD - NIGHT

As they see the shutters close, people begin to cry and hold each other, then randomly and silently walk away, their arms around each other.

INT. DRAWING ROOM/PLAS NEWYDD - NIGHT

Sarah enters crying softly, and the Duke, who has been waiting, stands and takes her in his arms to comfort her.

INT. SCHOLARLY STUDY - DAY

An elderly pair of male hands search through the pages of a newspaper, and stop at the obituary column.

INSERT - OBITUARY COLUMN HEADING "BUTLER, LADY ELEANOR"

The hands holding the paper begin to tremble.

ELDERLY MALE VOICE
    "Butler, Lady Eleanor. Beloved Aunt of the Earls of Ormonde and Ossory, on June 2nd, 1829, in Llangollen, Wales. Survived by her lifelong companion..."

The camera pulls back to reveal an aged Nigel in his clerical clothing. His now shaking hands crumble the newspaper, and he looks up, distraught.

NIGEL
    How long has it been? Fifty years! Dear God, what have I done? I refuted a desperate loving act with an anger that has lasted my entire life.

Nigel begins to cry, then gets control of himself, and looks up, determined.

EXT. COUNTRY ROAD/WALES - DAY

Nigel is being driven in a chaise by a 62 year old ADULT TIMOTHY.

NIGEL

You know Llangollen well, Timothy?

TIMOTHY

I do, sir. I've lived here all my life.

NIGEL

Then you would know Lady Eleanor Butler and her friend, Miss Ponsonby?

TIMOTHY

The Ladies? Aye. Everyone knows them.

Timothy's face distorts with grief, and he begins to cry. Nigel, taken aback, looks tactfully away.

TIMOTHY

But she has died you see. The Lady Eleanor. The town is not the same. And poor Miss Ponsonby. Desolate, it breaks the heart to see.

NIGEL

I hope to bring some comfort.

TIMOTHY

I hope you do, sir, for no one is more deserving.

They ride in silence until the chaise turns into the entrance of the beautiful present day Plas Newydd, now half timbered, with heavy Gothic decorations and windows.

TIMOTHY

This is Plas Newydd.

EXT. PLAS NEWYDD - DAY

Timothy disembarks and assists Nigel from the chaise. The porch and door are also heavily embellished with Gothic wood carvings. The door is opened by an aged and frail Mary Carryl.

TIMOTHY

Good day, Mary.

MARY CARRYL

Hello Timothy. Who have you brought?

TIMOTHY

An old acquaintance of Miss Sarah's. Come to pay his respects.

MARY CARRYL

Lovely. She's feeling a little better today. And you are Father...

NIGEL

If I may, I'll announce myself.

MARY CARRYL

Of course. This way, Father.

INT. DRAWING ROOM/PLAS NEWYDD - DAY

Sarah is seated near the fireplace. As Nigel enters and walks to the center of the room she looks up, recognition slowly dawning.

SARAH

Nigel?

Both Nigel's and Sarah's eyes fill with tears as he walks to sit on a footstool in front of her, taking her extended hands in his, and leaning forward to kiss them.

NIGEL

I'm so sorry, Sarah. So very, very sorry.

SARAH

Hush, Nigel. Be comforted. She didn't suffer... And she'll not be long without me.

NIGEL

(alarmed)
You aren't well?

SARAH

I'm prepared. One day follows another, each more empty than the previous.

NIGEL

I've come to ask your forgiveness.

SARAH

We forgave you long ago.

NIGEL

I didn't deserve it. Such cruel insensitivity, from one who loved you so much. And still does.

SARAH

Dearest Nigel. Those who love are so vulnerable. It's they who suffer most. We understood.

Sarah stands shakily and Nigel gets to his feet to assist her.

SARAH

Let me show you our home, then we'll talk of old times and old friends, and fill in the events of the years we haven't shared.

EXT. PLAS NEWYDD - DAY

A chaise bearing Nigel is leaving Plas Newydd. The house is seen in the background, with Mary Carryl and Sarah standing at the front door, waving as it drives out of sight.

NIGEL (VO)

I lost my beautiful Sarah for the second time on December 8th, 1831. Her precious heart could support her grief no longer. The wait to join her beloved Eleanor was a scant 18 months, longer than she had wished, but God will not be rushed. They lie now together forever in Llangollen, their faithful Mary Carryl but a short distance away.

CU - NIGEL'S TEAR STAINED FACE - DAY

NIGEL (VO)

For my own part, I acknowledge that I was young and ignorant of life, and have accepted my rage as a natural consequence of the fear and prejudice attendant on such ignorance. Yet I do not forgive myself. Grace is in God's domain, not mine.

FLASHBACK

Slow motion repeat and extension of the early scene of Eleanor and Sarah suffused in sunlight, crossing the bridge in Kilkenny, as seen by Nigel near the start of the film.

NIGEL (VO)

In my dreams, and waking, I see them still. Young, vibrant, and happy. On the brink of that glorious union which was to last for over half a century. A commitment in loving that may serve as an example for all of us.

CLOSING CREDITS

FADE OUT

The Real Story of
The Ladies' Lives

Eleanor Butler was born in 1739, most probably in Cambrai, France, where the Butlers had relatives. She was not the only offspring of Lord Walter and Lady Butler, but had two older sisters and a younger brother, John, who was to inherit the family properties. Walter Butler, Eleanor's father, was a very distant and impoverished cousin of the Dukes of Ormonde, and it was only by a twist of fate that he unexpectedly inherited Kilkenny Castle where Eleanor spent her early years. The family titles had been stripped some 20 years previously from the 2nd Duke of Ormonde, who had been accused of treason by his monarch, and they were not actually restored until 1791 to Eleanor's younger brother, John. Thus it was not until 1791 that Eleanor officially obtained the title of "Lady" which was used throughout the screenplay.

In the post-Cromwellian society which prevailed at that time in Ireland, adoption of the Church of England (Anglican) religion was a political and economic necessity. In spite of this, Madam Butler, as Eleanor's mother wished to be addressed, remained a staunch and public Roman Catholic. Since the Butlers were not well-off financially this added to the family's difficult economic circumstances. Madam Butler is described as proud and overbearing, and Walter Butler as completely governed by her whims.

At about the age of 13 Eleanor was sent to a convent at Cambrai to be educated; an experience she loved and spoke gratefully of throughout her life. France at the time was entering the Age of Enlightenment, a period of great intellectual activity in the humanities and science, initiated in large part by the French author Jean Jacques Rousseau. It was from this early exposure in Cambrai that Eleanor developed a passionate life-long interest in both Rousseau's literary works and his life. Several reliable accounts also reveal that French convents were places where sexual as well as intellectual enlightenment had definitely arrived. Not only did many of the nuns have male lovers, but lesbianism (sapphism) was so common that it was not considered significant enough to warrant a trip to the confessional. So, in view of her liberal education, Eleanor's return to the modest town of Kilkenny at about the age of 16, after the excitement of France, must have been stifling.

Sarah was born in 1755. Her early childhood was very unfortunate and unhappy. Her mother did die when she was only two or three, and her father a few years later. She then lived with a stepmother who died when Sarah was 13. It was at this point that Sarah was sent to live with Lady Betty and Sir William Fownes at their home, Woodstock, in Innistiogue, a beautiful Georgian house with extravagant gardens. Lady Betty's only child, a daughter also named Sarah, had been married a few years previously and lived some distance away.

All descriptions of Lady Betty depict her as being sweet-natured and generous. Sir William is described as a man with a nasty disposition, who treated his wife with a lack of respect bordering on cruelty. The Fownes were well off and also owned a home in a fashionable part of Dublin, where they went for the theater season and where Lady Betty's lifelong friend, Mrs. Lucy Goddard, also made her home. Lucy Goddard played a much larger part in The Ladies' story than the screenplay portrays. She was an intimate friend not only of Lady Betty but also of Sarah, and they corresponded frequently. It was from the letters which Mrs. Goddard saved from Sarah and Lady Betty and in her own diaries that most of the details of the elopement were preserved.

It must have been shortly after her arrival at Woodstock that Sarah was sent to Parke School in Kilkenny, whose screenplay headmistress, Beatrice, is imaginary. Particulars of Sarah's abrupt departure from Woodstock to Kilkenny are unknown. It is also not known how Sarah and Eleanor met, but they appear to have become friends early after Sarah's arrival. Eleanor was at the time about 29 to Sarah's 13, there actually being some 16 years difference in their ages. The details of Eleanor's tutoring of Sarah are also imaginary, although they must have been extensive, if informal, given the brevity of Sarah's education at Parke School and her later intellectual competencies. Sarah's few years in Kilkenny cemented their friendship, which was continued by letters and visits in both directions after Sarah's return to Woodstock.

Thus the lives of these two friends continued for some seven or eight years until 1778, when the famous elopement was executed. Both Eleanor and Sarah had been very unhappy for some time. In fact, desperate would be a more apt description. Eleanor's mother had been putting unrelenting pressure on her now 39 year old spinster daughter, who had no recorded proposals of marriage, to return to the convent at Cambrai permanently. Sarah was now 23, strikingly beautiful, and had already reportedly turned down two suitors. Lady Betty's health was failing, and Sir William, anxious to sire a male heir, was making very definite and persistent advances to Sarah. It was with difficulty that Sarah concealed this fact from Lady Betty, of whom she said she would rather die than emotionally wound. Instead she confided her anguish in letters to her friend, Mrs. Goddard.

Thus the threats to both Sarah and Eleanor were severe, and strong enough to force them to look for plausible alternatives to staying where they were. But to elope? No precedent of female elopement existed in 1778, and Eleanor and

The cover pastel painting of Valle Crucis Abbey ruins, by Jane Morris Pack, a teacher at the Aegean Center for the Fine Arts, on the island of Paros, Cyclades, Greece. Jane, a 20 year friend of book designer Stephen Harrison, became interested in The Ladies and this publication on hearing about it from him, and was inspired to do this beautiful cover. And, while Stephen was still worrying about how to get the painting safely to the US from that tiny Greek island, FedEx delivered it to his office. No customs, no fuss, in perfect shape. "God," as Eleanor might say, "is not unkind."

◆

Top. The cottage when The Ladies first rented it in 1779. Its age at that time is unknown. It was indeed "perceived to be outside the town" as they are told by the rental agent in the film, Evan Pugh. Evan Pugh is the name of my first maternal forebear to emigrate to Newfoundland from Wales: my great, great, great grandfather. I like to think that some of my ancestors may have known of The Ladies, and that my association with them is in some way a revisitation by a different generation. But then, as you may already have suspected, I am an incurable romantic. The ruins of Dinas Bran can be seen on the distant hill-top.

Bottom. The transformation to the Plas Newydd of today was accomplished gradually, by The Ladies over their 50 year residency, and by successive owners. The most dramatic changes were added between 1876-80 by General John Yorke, who had actually met The Ladies when a child. General Yorke commanded the Royal Dragoons at Balaclava, of Crimean war and Florence Nightingale fame. As an aside, in the United Kingdom Miss Nightingale is also revered for her initiation of and participation in legislation to restore the health and efficiency of, and hospital care for the British military, which had declined seriously since Waterloo and the Duke of Wellington's dominion. How close are the circles of life and fate, "to be sure," again as Eleanor might have reflected.

Top. In this photo there is a much better view of the decorative and striking half-timbering of the exterior of Plas Newydd, added by General Yorke, which makes such an impact on first sight of the house. Also notice the large stones in the foreground, which are representative of a circle of bardic stones dedicated to Welsh poets used in the 1908 Llangollen National Eisteddfod. This music festival, now international in scope, is held each year in July, and attracts some 100,000 visitors. Plas Newydd's visitors number upwards of 50,000 per year, many probably discovering it coincidentally to festival attendance.

PLAS NEWYDD
- HOUSE OF THE LADIES -
OPEN TO THE PUBLIC

APRIL:-
MON - SAT   10AM - 5PM
SUNDAY   10AM - 4PM

MAY TO SEPTEMBER:-
MON - SAT   10AM - 7PM
SUNDAY   10AM - 5PM

OCTOBER:-
MON - SAT   10AM - 5PM
SUNDAY   10AM - 4PM

ENTRANCE ➡

LIMITED CAR PARKING FOR VISITORS

Photo Credits (both): Laurie Menday

Bottom. This is the sign that greeted visitors to Plas Newydd in 1993, at the top of Butler Hill, a very appropriately named thoroughfare.

Photo Credits (both): Photographs by Mike Flory. Used by permission of Clwyd District Council, Ruthin, Clwyd

Top. The imposing exterior of Plas Newydd makes the house look quite large, but as you can see from the contrast with the visitors in this photo, looks are deceiving. It feels small upon entering. The ceilings, predictably for the age of the house, are low, and the rooms are not large. The "State Bedchamber," as The Ladies facetiously called their guest bedroom, is scarcely bigger than a large closet. An excellent audio-tape guide is provided to point out the many interesting features of the house, and to give facts about The Ladies' lives, and their many visitors.

Bottom. The front door and porch of Plas Newydd, whose completion delighted The Ladies so much that they held a "porch warming" party for selected friends. The uprights are bedposts dating from the 1600s, and two wood carved lions located here were a gift from the Duke of Wellington. The door portrays the four evangelists: Matthew, Mark, Luke and John, and includes several inscriptions, one of which reads "Watch, for you know not the houre!" The entrance provides the first close up view of the gothic carvings which so dominate the interior.

Photo Credits (both): Photographs by Mike Flary. Used by permission of Glyndwr District Council, Ruthin, Clwyd

The foyer of Plas Newydd looking toward the front door. Eleanor and Sarah were very proud of the black and white stone tiles they added here in 1788. The gothic carvings of the interior are, as can be seen, resplendent. Reputed to be one of the finest examples of gothic decoration in the United Kingdom, they would take days to examine in detail. However, the audio-tape guide does an excellent job of pointing out the most famous pieces. The Ladies are reputed to have enlisted the help of their friends in adding to this passion for carvings, and many are identified as having been gifts from famous visitors.

Photo Credits (both): Photographs by Mike Flory. Used by permission of Glyndwr District Council, Ruthin, Clwy

Top. The Ladies' bed chamber. Not their original bed, which was described to have been as ornately carved as the gothic interior of the house. In this photo the room is quite empty. In The Ladies' time it was described as being so cluttered with gifts and objects that people wondered how Eleanor and Sarah could navigate without knocking things over. The oriole windows were added by The Ladies, and give a greater sense of space to the small rooms, not to mention more light. As you can see there are no shutters on the windows, belying the screenplay scene where Sarah closes the shutters at Eleanor's death to signal the mourners waiting outside in the cold, dark evening of her passing.

Bottom. These embroidered slippers date from The Ladies' era. Sarah, in life as well as in the screenplay, loved needlework. Hopefully its pursuit allowed her mind to be "filled with dreams, and plans, and happy thoughts," as she says when a child in one of her early screenplay scenes. One room of the house is devoted to artifacts representative of the years in which The Ladies lived.

Photo Credits (both): Photographs by Mike Flere. Used by permission of Glyndwr District Council, Ruthin, Clwyd

Top. The dining room of Plas Newydd, where the numerous famous people who traveled to see The Ladies dined with them. Eleanor was very proud of the fact that she and Sarah could provide an entire meal from their own gardens and livestock, as well she should have been. Notice the harp to the left in the photo. The Ladies kept a harp in the house, and on occasion they would set it to catch the wind and howl at night to mystify overnight guests. Some of the stained glass in the windows of Plas Newydd was reputedly taken from the ruins of Valle Crucis Abbey.

Bottom. This painting is not known to have belonged to The Ladies, but would be similar to those they owned. They had numerous pets, and their affection for the dog, Frisk, early in the screenplay, is in no way fabricated. They had a strong affection also for their livestock, no doubt due to their total understanding of how vital these creatures were to their personal survival.

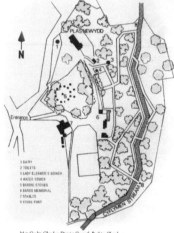

Plas Newydd Llangollen

1 DAIRY
2 TOILETS
3 LADY ELEANOR'S BOWER
4 WATER TOWER
5 BARDIC STONES
6 BARDS MEMORIAL
7 STABLES
8 STONE FONT

PLASNEWYDD

N

Entrance

CYFLYMEN STREAM

Map Credit: Glyndwr District Council, Ruthin, Clwyd

The present day formal gardens of Plas Newydd were first created in 1890 by two Liverpool cotton brokers, H.R. and G.H.F. Robertson, who owned the house for some years. In Eleanor and Sarah's lifetime the gardens were comprised of gravel paths leading to romantic vistas, rustic seats and a summerhouse. Their landscaping consisted primarily of shrubs and trees, flowers in profusion, and separate fruit tree and vegetable gardens. The present day topiary, while beautiful in these photos, has to be walked through to be truly appreciated. The map shows the relative size of the current 12 acre estate. Plas Newydd is top left, and the Cyflymen stream borders on the right. The estate became a property of the Llangollen Urban District Council in 1932, and remains an historic site.

A stone bridge which crosses the Cyflymen stream behind Plas Newydd today. During The Ladies' tenure they erected several wooden bridges across the stream, thus providing the "rustic bridge over a rushing stream" for the screenplay scene where Arthur is tossed from his pony while crossing it. Poetic license at work. One of Lady Eleanor's rustic bowers, or retreats, was in this area overlooking the Cyflymen. The walk along its banks is still serene and beautiful. It was one of The Ladies' favorite evening strolls.

St. Collen's church in Llangollen, which dates from the late 6th or early 7th century. Llangollen actually translates into English as "St. Collen's church." Collen was a monk who lived in this location in the 6th century. He had previously been a soldier, and his sainthood seems to relate to an ancient Welsh myth or "Faery" story about his bravery as a soldier in defeating a demon king. The oak ceiling of St. Collen's is thought to date from the 7th century, and many other artifacts within the church are equally as ancient. Eleanor, Sarah and Mary Carryl are buried just outside the entrance to St. Collen's. Their tomb is still intact, and contains several unusual inscriptions which visitors delight in reading.

In the screenplay, Sarah makes a life saving visit to the vicar of St. Collen's, Mr. Protherow, to ask his help in hiring a workman, because she and Eleanor are shunned on their arrival in Llangollen by the entire town. This is pure fiction, as no early information survives on their initial social acceptance.

Photo Credit: Laurie Monday

Valle Crucis Abbey is quite real, and very special. It was built about 1200 by a Welsh chieftain nan ed Madoc, the ruins of whose fortress, Dinas Bran, Eleanor and Sarah explore on their first day in the Dee Valley. It is at Valle Crucis that the screenplay's introductory party is given for Eleanor and Sarah by Lady Dungannon, and they wear for the first time their famous black habits. Lady Dungannon, the real life grandmother of the Duke of Wellington, was a personal friend of The Ladies for many years, and was responsible for introducing them to many of the local gentry.

This is the photo of the Valle Crucis which inspired Jane Morris Pack to paint the cover for Love, above the reach of time. The Abbey was home to a branch of the austere Cistercian monks until its abandonment in 1535. The ruins are quite extensive, and include a particularly beautiful chapter house, which remains in pristine condition. The Abbey is otherworldly, and located in an indescribably beautiful Dee Valley setting.

Yours truly, in a contemplative mood at Valle Crucis Abbey, just minutes after The Ladies became, unbeknownst to me at the time, a major focus of my life. The Abbey lies about a mile and a half to the north of the town; a gentle walk along an ancient canal. Valle Crucis is a sacred space, at least it was for me, which is why I made it so in the screenplay for Eleanor and Sarah, when they walk through it for the first time and sense its "aura." I have only to think of Valle Crucis to regain the emotions I felt while there. This is not a statement I can make about too many places I have seen in the world, and I have been fortunate enough to have visited many.

Photo Credit: Rick Stankmann Photography

Many souvenirs were produced in their lifetime which featured The Ladies. This 5½ inch high porcelain figurine probably dates from the late 1700s. I saw one like it in Llangollen in 1993, but did not even inquire about the price. This one, miraculously I feel, came into my life in my home town of St. John's, Newfoundland, during a visit there in 1999, when I was doing my ritual tour of local antique and curio shops with my lifelong friend, Midge Kerr. Midge, who never misses anything, totally missed this one. Not even registering the significance of my find, I did not buy the figurine until the following day, at Midge's urging, for $40 Canadian ($25 US). The Ladies' famous black habits, which were popular for fox hunting, were only briefly in vogue in England. Did they adopt this style deliberately to look different? Eleanor implies this in her response to Sarah's "I've never seen anything like it. It's very different," by saying "We're different ... We should be distinctive." A more likely reason is their financial constraints, since it eliminated any need to keep up with the latest fashions.

◆

This postcard probably dates from the late 1800s or early 1900s. The Ladies would not allow themselves to be painted in their lifetime. Their facial likenesses were painted surreptitiously by a friend when Eleanor was in her late 80s, and already blind. The original small watercolor painting of them hangs in the living room of Plas Newydd. The identity of the artist who used The Ladies' facial likenesses in this scene, which became the most famous of them, is not known. Sarah, who was taller than Eleanor, would be on the left. The Ladies wore their hair cropped short and powdered long after this style went out of fashion. In an 1818 account of his travels on foot in Wales, a gentleman named Mr. G.H. Steele described The Ladies as "in every respect resembling the Man of fashion as far as respects Dress." Much thanks to my friend Sidney Goodman, who, intrigued by my "Ladies" project, tracked this card down on e-bay for me, as well as a Llangollen travel guide dated 1934, from which I obtained a great deal of new information on Dinas Bran and Valle Crucis.

◆

This beautiful enameled brooch showing The Ladies measures 1¼ inch by 1 inch. It probably also dates from the late 1700s. It was discovered by my friend, David Templeton, at a "jumble" sale at the church of my childhood, St. Andrew's Presbyterian: The "Kirk," in St. John's. David found this about two months after I found the figurine. All my friends were aware of my screenplay, as it was under production option at the time of my prior year's visit, when I had spent two weeks there doing some rewrites of the script. As equally incredible as the brooch's discovery by David was his persistence in waiting a year and a half until my next visit home to give it to me. He wore it on the lapel of his jacket to a party, and asked me what I thought of it. I was beyond thought. I was in total shock. I had heard of The Ladies having been honored on two sets of tableware and knew about the figurine, but never a mention of a brooch. Omens, anyone? Thank you, David, for one of the truly magic moments of my life.

Sarah's was to become the first of record; reason enough for the international curiosity the event sparked. But precedent is only one factor in elopement. Consider the impediments The Ladies faced. They had no one to flee to, no money, no way to earn a living, and no prospects of financial support from either of their families. Elopement takes great passion as well as unusual circumstances, and that passion existed was to be borne out by events as they unfolded.

With the help of Mary Carryl, who was a servant at Woodstock, The Ladies executed the elopement after dark one early Spring night in 1778. Details of the elopement abound in biographical information on The Ladies, but they are obscured by conflicting accounts. It is definitely known that The Ladies wore men's clothing; they did take the dog Frisk with them (because it barked?); they either escaped on horseback or they did not; they carried a gun, or they had none; they spent a week traveling to Waterford, walking by night and resting by day, or they got there much sooner. So the conflicting stories go. What history has glossed over is the far more important fact that the elopement was a failure.

Sarah left a note for Lady Betty's married daughter, Sarah Tighe, who was visiting Woodstock at the time. As soon as it and The Ladies' absence was discovered, Sir William began frantically combing the countryside in an attempt to locate them. It was days before The Ladies were apprehended near Waterford. In one version The Ladies were exposed by the barking of Frisk, and discovered hiding in a barn. Members of both families are reported to have arrived on the scene in separate coaches almost simultaneously. A heated interchange ensued, with Sarah and Eleanor declaring their determination not to be stopped in their plans to leave Ireland and live together, and the families just as vociferously demanding they surrender. But Sarah had caught a severe cold and was quite ill, and The Ladies were forced to relent. Sarah was taken back to Woodstock, and Eleanor to the home of a married sister, where she was virtually imprisoned.

Now the aborted elopement picks up momentum. For a week or so frantic letters flew back and forth between The Ladies, and between Lady Betty and Sarah and Mrs. Goddard, who was in Dublin. Sarah had recovered physically by then, but was deeply depressed and emotionally distraught, which was caus-ing Lady Betty great alarm. Sarah declared that she loved Eleanor, and that she was determined to live and die with her. It was at this juncture that Eleanor's sister reported that Eleanor had disappeared. For several days her whereabouts were unknown, until Sir William is reported to have been approached by a stranger who told him that Eleanor was concealed at Woodstock! And indeed she was, in Sarah's bedroom, with the help of Mary Carryl.

Sir William demanded that the Butlers come for Eleanor, but by this time they had had enough scandal, and wanted nothing more than to be rid of their rebellious daughter. The elopement, which was initially viewed as nothing more than a frivolous escapade of romantic friendship since no men were involved, had taken on a new and unacceptable significance for both families. Eleanor was frequently described as masculine and satirical in manner, and there was the widespread knowledge of same sex female relationships to consider. Word had also begun to leak out of Sir William's attentions to Sarah, which began to put unbearable strain on the situation at Woodstock.

At this point Mrs. Goddard arrived from Dublin, intent on persuading Sarah that Eleanor was an unfit companion, and that Sarah should give up any idea of being able to live contentedly with her. Sarah adamantly and hysterically refused to listen to any criticism of Eleanor, whom she unhesitatingly declared she loved, and the intractability of her attachment and Eleanor's determination finally won the day. Arrangements were made to let The Ladies go. Walter Butler sent his solicitor to arrange a stipend, and on the morning of May 4th, 1778, Sarah and Eleanor left Woodstock in high spirits. They departed in style, by coach, accompanied as befitted ladies of their rank by a servant, the ever faithful Mary Carryl. There is no subsequent mention of poor Frisk, and his part in The Ladies' story ends here.

Almost unbelievable tragedy followed at Woodstock after The Ladies' departure. At the end of May Sir William became extremely ill, and after suffering abominably for upwards of a week died in great agony. Mrs. Goddard records that Sir William was convinced his agony was caused by his misbehavior toward Sarah, an idea with which Mrs. Goddard herself seems to have taunted him. Less than a month later, Mrs. Goddard, back in Dublin, received word of Lady Betty's death. She had always been described as frail, but the cause of her death is unrecorded. So in little more than a month, and long before Eleanor and Sarah had an opportunity to receive any news from Ireland, both Sir William and Lady Betty Fownes were dead and buried.

The Ladies' mood of adventurous travel in the early part of their trip soon changed to one of concern as money became tight. They passed through Llangollen, which they apparently both loved at first sight, but according to plan they traveled on to spend their first winter in England. However, England was very expensive, and consequently they returned to Wales the following spring, where the cost of living was affordable. They are reputed never again to have left their chosen village of Llangollen for longer than an overnight visit elsewhere. Their cottage, which they did name Plas Newydd, was quite small and insignificant when they first rented it. But immediately, and over the course of their 50 years together there, they began to develop their beautiful and increasingly famous gardens, and to enlarge and improve the cottage. They were also determined to improve their minds, and continued to be voracious readers in French, Spanish and Italian. They devoted hours every day to their studies, and recorded reading a staggering number of books each month. They also managed to keep up to date on the latest news of the day worldwide, from newspapers if it was in print, but increasingly by virtue of the information and gossip passed along by their multitude of visitors. In truth, as has been frequently written of them, they seemed to know everyone and everything of importance.

There seems little doubt that Mary Carryl was the greatest asset in The Ladies' early survival. Described as tall and gaunt, she had a very forceful personality to say the least, having been called "Mollie the Bruiser" for throwing a candlestick at a fellow servant in employment previous to her Woodstock days. It is Mary who bargained with the local merchants as Eleanor wrote on one occasion, "Loud and violent altercation between Mary and the Fisherman. Mary Triumphant." *The Hamwood Papers of The Ladies of Llangollen and Caroline Hamilton.* Mary also continued to care for The Ladies as much as possible in their accustomed style, because there is no indication that Eleanor or Sarah planted anything other than flowers, although they oversaw all that was done at Plas Newydd, and Eleanor does seem to have had knowledge of farming practices and animals.

Located in northeastern Wales near the English border, Llangollen was a common overnight stopping place on the heavily traveled stagecoach route between Ireland and London. Thus The Ladies' fame was initiated, at least in part, by curious travelers passing through the village, who not infrequently intruded on their privacy unannounced. While the well publicized elopement most likely was the initial attraction, The Ladies also epitomized in the public mind the then current romanticism of personal withdrawal from society to a rural setting, there to commune with nature and devote one's life to intellectual pursuits and thoughts. Henry David Thoreau was to do the same some sixty years later in the USA, when he retreated to Walden Pond for two years. These facts notwithstanding, there is little doubt that it was news of The Ladies' sparkling personalities, intelligence, and graciousness which ultimately attracted the interest of the more famous personages who traveled to meet them, and returned time and again as cherished friends.

The Duke of Wellington was introduced to The Ladies while still a young man by his maternal grandmother, Lady Dungannon, whose estate, Brynkinalt, was not too far distant from Llangollen. Lady Dungannon seems to have been one of their earliest friends and champions, and she took pains to introduce The Ladies to the gentry living nearby. The Ladies did not, however, rescue the Duke of Wellington from a raging stream when he was a child, and thus inadvertently contribute to the overthrow of Emperor Napoleon. But the Duke, who became a close personal friend, corresponded with them throughout their lives, and took every opportunity to visit.

The private reality of The Ladies' lives, however, is that they lived on the edge of poverty. They had only sporadic financial support from relatives, and it is assumed also from friends. In later years Eleanor received a small state pension, which greatly helped them in their declining years. They were particularly sensitive to their inability to pay the bills of the honest and hardworking tradespeople who gave them credit. In Eleanor's journal/day books, she frequently writes of the anguish of being unable to pay small bills, or her relief in being able to do so: "Man came with a Bill for so small a sum that we were distressed at not being able to pay him;" "our Landlord came. Paid him his half year's rent, which was due last November but we had not money;" "The Coal man came with his bill ... Thank heaven we had the money to pay him." *The Hamwood Papers.* Their own financial hardship made them particularly sensitive to the fate of others less fortunate, and when they could, they gave. Their financial problems were not helped by the fact that they had very expensive upper class tastes. Everything they owned was personalized with their initials, including stationery, china and crystal, and their expenses for book purchases were astonishing. One area where they did economize was in clothing. The black tuxedo type habits they adopted provided them with a distinctive look and appearance at minimal cost. It eliminated the necessity to keep up with fashion, which they could ill afford to do. It also made them, especially as they aged, look increasingly eccentric and masculine, which seemed not to embarrass them in the least.

What was the local townspeople's reaction to these strange foreign ladies? No details of early impressions survive, but once The Ladies' visitors began to arrive they brought welcome and important trade to the village. Not the least to profit from this traffic was Edwards of the Hand Hotel, with whom Eleanor had ongoing upsets. Sarah, the quieter of the two, was the peacemaker when Eleanor's hot temper caused occasional upsets with the locals, or less often with friends. Over time The Ladies are described as being treated like royalty in Llangollen, where they were consulted on and involved in decision making for the entire community.

This good will did not extend universally, and the *General Evening Post* article of July 1780, just two years after their elopement, was a devastating blow to them. It seems ridiculous to think that their sexuality would not be an issue. With knowledge of same sex female relationships so widespread, and The Ladies' public unreserved display of their love and devotion to each other, it was bound to be suspected. However, no information survives which suggests that their sexual orientation seemed to matter to the townspeople. Their friends also loved and cherished them, and their lives went on.

Mary Carryl was the first to die, after a long and wasting illness suggestive of cancer, in 1809. She left her life savings to Sarah, which provided The Ladies with the purchase price of a field next to their cottage. This added significantly to acreage they had previously rented and hired laborers to farm. Thus The Ladies did indirectly become farmers early in their Llangollen life, and their financial hardships were at least slightly ameliorated from this income source. Eleanor lived to be 90, and died quietly of old age at Plas Newydd in 1829. The townspeople are reported to have been devastated by the death of their venerated Lady Eleanor. Sarah was not well, and did not attend the burial. At her death Eleanor's small state pension terminated, and it was due to the Duke of Wellington's petitioning first the Prime Minister, then the King of England, that it was continued for Sarah for the balance of her life. Sarah lived quietly for only 18 months after Eleanor's death, when she appears to have died of congestive heart failure. She was 78. She was buried as planned beside her beloved Eleanor in St. Collen's churchyard, and their devoted Mary Carryl does indeed lie nearby.

Two of the most significant characters in the screenplay, Sir Geoffrey Bannister and Nigel Davenport, are fictitious. Writing is a strange and wonderful experience, and as the screenplay progressed these gentle men became as real as did the flesh and blood people in The Ladies' lives. It is in verbal interchange with close friends that the personalities of the main characters in a screenplay are most fully revealed, and Geoffrey and Nigel played their parts magnificently in this role. It would be nice to think that The Ladies had such wonderful intimate friends in their early lives, but information on their friendships in this period is totally absent.

At their deaths The Ladies' entire personal effects and house were sold at auction. Plas Newydd today is owned and operated as an Historic Site by the Welsh Denbighshire County Council. The cottage was extensively changed by a subsequent owner, General York, who added the picturesque half timbering of the exterior and many of the gothic wood carvings of the interior, following the style adopted by The Ladies from 1798 onwards. But for the most part the house remains as they last knew it, surrounded by beautiful if significantly different gardens, the Cyflymen stream flowing gently behind it, the ruins of Castle Dinas Bran silhouetted high atop a hill in the background, and Valle Crucis Abbey but a short and delightful walk away.

A Selected Bibliography
that Continues The Ladies' Story

Plas Newydd and the Ladies of Llangollen. Glyndwr District Council: Ruthin, Clwyd, Wales. 1988

This is a colorful and chock-full of facts sixteen page free booklet about The Ladies and Plas Newydd that I picked up when I visited Llangollen in 1993. Pick up an updated copy at Plas Newydd when you go to visit the Ladies' home, Llangollen and the surrounding area. It's all exquisitely beautiful. Be sure to include a visit to the nearby English cathedral towns of Chester and Lincoln on your trip.

The Hamwood Papers of The Ladies of Llangollen and Caroline Hamilton. Edited by Mrs. G.H. Bell. Macmillan and Co.: London. 1930

This work is available only in libraries. Caroline Hamilton was the granddaughter of Lady Betty. It consists of Caroline's recollections of the stories her mother, Sarah Fownes Tighe, told Caroline about The Ladies, the content of letters between Sarah, Lady Betty, and Mrs. Goddard concerning the elopement, historical facts about The Ladies and their families, and excerpts from Eleanor's day books. As the original source material on the elopement, it is often a fascinating read, but some parts may be tedious. Depends on your scholastic interests.

The Ladies of Llangollen. Elizabeth Mavor. Penguin Books: London. 1971

This is an in-depth scholarly biography of The Ladies' lives. It includes many references to the history, politics, literary personages and literature of The Ladies' era, and many details of their friendships after they settled in Llangollen. It presents The Ladies as romantic friends only; the author negates the possibility that a lesbian relationship existed between them. A work of six years research and writing, it provides details not found elsewhere, including the fact, which I discovered after I had invented a possibly lesbian ancestor for Eleanor, that she did indeed have a warrior ancestress. This book also includes many engravings and portraits of The Ladies, members of their families, and Plas Newydd at various stages of its enlargement. A very touching and beautiful song (poem) from a source identified by the author as Mrs. Carter's Letters to Miss C. Talbot (1809), v.1, p. 57., which Sarah wrote describing her love for Eleanor, reproduced below, appears in Ms. Mavor's excellent biography.

By Vulgar Eros long misled
I call'd thee Tyrant, mighty love!
With idle fears my fancy fled
Nor ev'ne thy pleasures wish'd to prove.

Condem'd at length to wear thy chains
Trembling I felt and ow'd thy might
But soon I found my fears were vain
Soon hugg'd my chain, and thought it light.

Passions Between Women. Emma Donoghue. Scarlet Press: London. 1993 and HarperCollins: New York. 1995

Ms Donohue set out to research lesbian references in British literature between 1668 and 1801 as part of her doctoral studies. It is as a result of the voluminous literature she uncovered and has carefully documented that I have felt free to include such bold statements about historical lesbian relationships in the text of this book. There is little doubt that Eleanor and Sarah, being the voracious readers they were, were familiar with much of this information. Indeed Eleanor listed many of the same titles in some of her ongoing lists of books read. It is also from Passions Between Women that Hester Thrale Piozzi's diary entry revealing The Ladies' lesbian orientation was quoted. Fascinating reading.

I Know My Own Heart: The Diaries of Anne Lister 1791-1840. Edited by Helena Whitbread. Virago: London. 1988, and New York University Press: NY. 1992 and

No Priest But Love: The Journals of Anne Lister from 1824-1826. Edited by Helena Whitbread. New York University Press: NY. 1992

Anne Lister was an English noblewoman who was also a lesbian. She kept diaries in a code of her own design which Helena Whitbread has painstakingly deciphered and edited. These works dispel any notion that noblewomen in these years were ignorant of their sexuality, and lesbian sexuality in particular. The number of encounters Anne reports is quite impressive. Anne also made a trip from her home near York, England, to visit The Ladies in Llangollen in July of 1822, specifically to try to determine if they were " like" her, in other words, lesbian, a term, however, with which Anne was unfamiliar. She gives a detailed description of Plas Newydd and its grounds, the countryside around Llangollen, her meeting with Sarah, encounters with townspeople and their devotion to The Ladies, and a visit to Dinas Bran. Eleanor was ill at the time of her visit and Anne did not meet her; I Know My Own Heart, pages 188-215. The content on The Ladies alone is worth the price of this particular journal.

Also of interest is Mrs. Whitbread's choice of the title, "I Know My Own Heart." It is part of a quotation in J.J. Rousseau's Confessions, Volume 1. *To wit: "I know my own heart & I know men. I am not like any other I have seen. I dare believe myself to be different from any others who exist." This is, of course, the same Jean Jacques Rousseau of Eleanor's passion. Draw your own conclusions, I certainly enjoy my own.*

La Nouvelle Héloïse (Julie, or, The New Eloise). Jean Jacques Rousseau. Translated and abridged by Judith H. McDowell. Pennsylvania State University Press: University Park, PA. 1968

This book, along with Samuel Richardson's Clarissa, *have the distinction of being identified as the first novels ever written, because they were the first to tell a story. Both did so in the form of letters between the main characters. It was from Rousseau's* La Nouvelle Héloïse *that the excerpts used in Eleanor and Sarah's last screenplay French lesson describing the affectionate friendship between Claire and Héloïse was taken. Both books are very much period pieces, and you may find them a dull read for other than historical purposes.*

Scotch Verdict. Lillian Faderman. Morrow: NY. 1983

A detailed and fascinating recounting of the 1815 Scottish trial on which Lillian Hellman's play and the film The Children's Hour *is based. A wonderful look at upper class Scottish/British male beliefs about, ignorance of, and attitudes toward lesbian relationships which still persisted in the later years of* The Ladies' *lives. An excellent read.*

Surpassing the Love of Men. Lillian Faderman. William Morrow: NY, 1981

An extensive research of the history of Romantic Friendships from the Renaissance to 1981. In this work Faderman presents romantic friendships, including The Ladies', *as a separate consideration from sexual intimacy. It was from reading about* The Ladies *in this work that my curiosity about them was sparked in the early 1980s.*

The School For Scandal and Other Plays. Richard Sheridan. Penguin Classics: NY. 1988

Now that you've discovered you enjoy reading plays you may want to read this one. Even if you've seen the play, which is still in regular production in some part of the world almost continuously (or so I've been told), reading the written version is even better than seeing the play. For one thing you don't miss any of the words. You'll remember from the screenplay that Eleanor and Sarah disagreed stongly over Mr. Sheridan's intent in writing this play, Eleanor being appalled at the harm done to perfectly innocent victims; Sarah treating it as a complete comedy. In the screenplay Eleanor and Sarah became victims of the same type of slander with The Evening Post's *attack on them. Eleanor at the time was 51, described as short and plump, just one glaring falsehood included in that particular article which was identified by their biographer, Elizabeth Mavor.*

Living In Sin: A Bishop Rethinks Human Sexuality. John Shelby Spong. Harper-Collins: San Francisco. 1988

Episcopalian Bishop John Spong (now retired) beautifully contrasts current scientific knowledge of human sexuality with its fundamentalist religious interpretation. He identifies with absolute clarity those biblical interpretations which perpetuate the sexual ignorance, fear and discrimination so rampant in current society. Homosexuality is but one of the many aspects of sexuality explored by this brilliant theological and scientific scholar and author. In his own words Bishop Spong states that "No aspect of our humanity is invested with more anxieties, yearnings, emotions, and needs than is our sexual nature. So, sex is a major area in which the prejudice of human beings finds expression." Living In Sin is, as the author states, a book about prejudice, not about sex. This book added much clarity to my understanding of sexual bigotry, and will to yours if you choose to read it.

What The Bible Really Says About Homosexuality. Daniel A. Helminiak, Ph.D. Alamo Square Press: San Francisco. 1994

Roman Catholic priest Daniel Helminiak revisits those biblical passages used to condemn homosexuality, and interprets them with meticulous detail to the context and times in which they were written. He examines all negative seeming verses, but does not forget to include discussion of positive references to homosexuality. His conclusion: "If people ... seek to know outright if gay or lesbian sex in itself is good or evil ... they will have to look elsewhere for an answer. For the fact of the matter is simple enough. The Bible never addresses the question. More than that, the Bible seems deliberately unconcerned about it." A book the open minded will learn much from; the prejudiced delight in attacking.

DaywalkS: Vale of Llangollen. Gordon Emery & John Roberts. Walkways: Birmingham. 1991

This guide contains maps and descriptions of 27 wonderful day walks which can be taken from Llangollen. In it I discovered the quote of a gentleman named G.H. Steele who met The Ladies while hiking through Llangollen in 1818. His interesting description of them is included as a photo caption in the photo section of the book.

Several fictional accounts have been written about The Ladies, but there are none to date that I feel do justice to the actual story of their lives.

Closing Credits

This is where I express my totally inadequate thanks to the principal people who have helped me realize this publication dream.

I am particularly indebted to author/researcher Dr. Lillian Faderman for directing me to the chief historical resources I used in my work; to David S. Freeman of Los Angeles, an outstanding screenwriting teacher, and to Michael Williams, David Collins, Dorothy Aufiero, and Annie Stevens of Scout Productions in Boston, and John G. Ives of Wayland, MA, talented film professionals all. Of my friends, I especially thank Laurie D. Munday, who first suggested I write about The Ladies, and suffered through countless rereads of the script at various stages; Alice Taylor Hanson, the ultimate critic of my grammatical and ecclesiastical errors, among innumerable other things; and Midge Kerr, who insisted on knowing the "whole" story of The Ladies' lives, and forced me to make the book as complete as it is. To my friend, Mark Willems, the talented renaissance artist who did the drawing of The Ladies for the screenplay's title page, no expression of gratitude can be sufficient. The unfailing personal support, encouragement and tremendous insights of these special friends brought the script to a level I could not have achieved alone. I very much appreciate the assistance of Rose McMahon, curator of Plas Newydd, in numerous small but vital details, and Avis Fenner, of Scarlet Press, London, for enlightening me on publication practices in the UK. In the book production phase I have been truly blessed by the talented Stephen Harrison and Louis Neiheisel of Peter T. Noble Associates, Encinitas, CA, and the marketing team of Carolyn Smith Konow and Judith Framan, of Framen & Smith Communications, San Diego, CA and Albuquerque, NM.

This book has been a labor of love on many levels besides my own, and my gratitude is boundless.

Fade Out

The end. Or is it?

Only time will tell. But one thing is for sure, if the screenplay is ever filmed it will be very different from its present form.

An original screenplay is called a spec script, and it is written to be read. It's quite different from a shooting script, which gives camera angles and other filming details, which will require significant changes. Also, when the dialogue is spoken it too will have to change. Actors become the person they portray, and they cannot possibly say everything exactly as I have written it. Those are just for starters. I don't even know how everything else would evolve, but I know that it would. I like to imagine that if the film is ever produced it will be even better than my screenplay. Why should it not, with the many wonderful talented people it could attract? But that's a distant dream, and having just fulfilled one, that of publication, I am totally content.

And now it's time to say good-bye. And to thank you for joining me on my journey with the endearing Ladies of Llangollen.